Dehydrated

Dehydrated

KAREN SCHATZLINE

CHARISMA
HOUSE

Most CHARISMA HOUSE BOOK GROUP products are available at special quantity discounts for bulk purchase for sales promotions, premiums, fund-raising, and educational needs. For details, write Charisma House Book Group, 600 Rinehart Road, Lake Mary, Florida 32746, or telephone (407) 333-0600.

DEHYDRATED by Karen Schatzline
Published by Charisma House
Charisma Media/Charisma House Book Group
600 Rinehart Road
Lake Mary, Florida 32746
www.charismahouse.com

Library of Congress Cataloging-in-Publication Data:
Schatzline, Karen.
  Dehydrated / by Karen Schatzline.
    pages cm
  Includes bibliographical references and index.
  ISBN 978-1-62998-620-3 (trade paper : alk. paper) -- ISBN 978-1-62998-621-0 (e-book)
  1. Spirituality--Christianity. 2. Spiritual life--Christianity. 3. Christian life. I. Title.
  BV4501.3.S3465 2015
  248.4--dc23
                          2015016884

There is nothing worse in life than loving God with all of your heart but then struggling to find the strength and motivation to live for Him daily. Karen Schatzline has generously shared the details of her journey to remind us all that God never designed us to function and operate in our human strength alone. We are instead created to be wholly dependent on Him and to practice a lifestyle of daily infilling of His grace, mercy, strength, power, and love. Without our daily "fill" of His presence through fresh and intimate encounters, we quickly discover the great in-built limitations of our humanity and inevitably lose our joy. This book instills hope that no matter what spiritual condition you find yourself in today, Jesus is waiting to saturate and rehydrate you with living water!

—RUSSELL EVANS
AUTHOR AND PASTOR, PLANETSHAKERS CHURCH, AUSTRALIA

If you are ready to discover a place of refreshing, life-giving water that will replenish and restore the life that you desire, get *Dehydrated*! Karen's inspirational message will lift you into new hope, joy, and peace for your journey.

—DAWN RALEY
COPASTOR, CALVARY CHURCH, ORMOND BEACH, FLORIDA

Dehydration in our physical bodies can be very dangerous! Spiritual dehydration can be even more dangerous! Spiritual dehydration's symptoms show up as hopelessness, shame, guilt, fears, addictions, negative thinking, unworthiness, thirsting for truth, weaknesses, anxiety, etc. God has given Karen revelatory and life-changing insight that can set you free from spiritual dehydration and put you on the road to recovery, spiritual healing, and a new beginning. This book is a spiritual fountain that will rehydrate your spiritual life to new levels.

—AL BRICE JR.
SENIOR PASTOR, COVENANT LOVE CHURCH
FAYETTEVILLE, NORTH CAROLINA

In *Dehydrated* Karen Schatzline brings us back to the Source—the One who offers not just any water, but the living water; the One who is not just a physician, but the Great Physician. The One who came so that we not only have life, but have it more abundantly. And the abundant life is the heart of this book. The God who healed still heals today, and the God who offered hope is still restoring hearts today. Drink deeply from the well, and finish strong!

—DAPHNE YANG
DEPUTY SENIOR PASTOR, CORNERSTONE COMMUNITY
CHURCH, SINGAPORE

Karen Schatzline is a voice to this generation. Her heart to see fresh encounters with the presence of God explodes through the pages of this book. Beware: after reading, you will never deny your thirst again!

—JOEL STOCKSTILL
EVANGELIST AND PROPHETIC VOICE, DALLAS, TEXAS

Many are believers; few become seekers. We sleepwalk our way through life redeemed, yet never revived from our slumber. This book not only exposes toxic thinking patterns that prevent us from receiving His life-giving power, but also unearths the benefits of a life spent in intimacy with the Father.

—CHRISTY JOHNSON
COPASTOR, FEARLESS CHURCH, LOS ANGELES, CALIFORNIA

Our generation has sadly exchanged the real "Jesus at the well" for cheap counterfeits that promise living water but leave us dangerously parched. In *Dehydrated* the Holy Spirit speaks through Karen Schatzline to lead us back to the well where a loving Savior patiently waits to give us a drink. Drinking from Jesus will replenish our spirits so that the seeds planted in the garden of our lives can flourish abundantly in every area. As you read this book, I pray that you respond to the call of the Lord to come and drink. He loves you more than you know!

—JOANN ROSARIO CONDREY
INTERNATIONAL WORSHIP LEADER AND PASTOR
RAINFIRE CHURCH, DOUGLASVILLE, GEORGIA

Karen is a warrior. She knows what it's like to go through times of deep sorrow and struggle. Yet, she has risen above it all because of her deep root system with Jesus. This book will do the same for you! It will enable your roots to go deep, and you will never be the same.

—DEBORAH BERTEAU
COPASTOR, THE HOUSE MODESTO, MODESTO, CALIFORNIA

Dehydrated truly captures the heartbeat of the Lord, desirous to give living water to all who thirst. Each chapter is an encouragement to rise up and allow the water of the Word and living waters of the Holy Spirit to quench, refresh, and overflow to and through every dehydrated soul so they may thirst no more!

—ANNE SPITSBERGEN
COLEAD PASTOR, ABIDING PLACE, SAN DIEGO, CALIFORNIA

Are you desiring to go to a new place of encounter with God? Are you thirsty for a fresh drink from His well? Are you desperate for more of His presence? *Dehydrated* by Karen Schatzline will take you to that place! It's a place where God is waiting for you! It's a place of intimacy, a place of refreshing, a place of suddenly finding yourself in His throne room with His love surrounding you. Karen Schatzline is one of the most amazing women of God I know! Her life epitomizes the love and character of God. In this book she unveils great revelation to all who want to know God more intimately, and great hope to all those who are discouraged! Let *Dehydrated* take you on a journey into the secret place with Him. Let it inspire you to become all that God wants you to become. Let it cause you to walk more securely in all that God has planned and destined for your life! This book will do just that. "Yet who knows whether you have come into the kingdom for such a time as this?" (Esther 4:14, NKJV).

—KATHIE THOMAS
COPASTOR, VICTORY CHRISTIAN CENTER
YOUNGSTOWN, OHIO

Have you ever just wanted something "more" to quench your thirst because what you were drinking wasn't working, wasn't satisfying, wasn't enough! You needed to "soak" your thirst with more. Karen Schatzline's book *Dehydrated* is that good "soak" that you are needing to satisfy your spiritual thirst with God! It will lead you to that place to drink and get soaked in His presence and glory! It will take you to a higher place in your hunger for His power. It will leave you changed and yet challenged to keep pursuing Him for more of that living water that quenches your spiritual want.

—PHYLLIS SAWYER
COLEAD PASTOR, CALVARY ASSEMBLY OF GOD
DECATUR, ALABAMA

Karen Schatzline's timely book *Dehydrated* couldn't be more appropriately titled. Just as even mild dehydration drains our energy and makes us tired, so neglect of spiritual hydration is marked by indications of decrease in our souls' zeal and stamina. Karen's candid diagnostic of a languishing church offers a viable prognosis if we will return to the well of His presence and drink deeply. These pages are filled with fountains of refreshing truths that will instantly revitalize the thirsty... and you'll never have to thirst again.

—TAVA BRICE
COPASTOR, COVENANT LOVE CHURCH
FAYETTEVILLE, NORTH CAROLINA

I have known Karen Schatzline for over fifteen years. If there is one phrase that would describe her it is:

"God-gifted encourager." We need voices such as hers in the body of Christ today that can speak to shame, guilt, and fear and cause them to turn into confidence, freedom, and faith! Karen does so in this book *Dehydrated*. If you have ever longed for a deeper relationship with Jesus that has substance and not shallowness, you will enjoy reading *Dehydrated*. You will become a more effective disciple of the Lord as you read with a heart that is open to change.

—KIM OWENS
COLEAD PASTOR, FRESH START CHURCH, PEORIA, ARIZONA

Karen's own personal, candid, and transparent experience is recanted in this powerful book. For those who may be hurting or discouraged, or for those who are simply hungry for more of Him, you will find a sense of hope within these pages. We have all been "dehydrated" at some point and Karen offers powerful insight to get us to the one true living "well."

—MICHELLE JONES
COLEAD PASTOR, TRINITY ASSEMBLY OF GOD
DELTONA, FLORIDA

Karen Schatzline brings fresh insight and inspiration to the body of Christ for the much needed drink of living water. Prepare to be refreshed.

—LESLIE CRANDALL
SENIOR ASSOCIATE OVERSEER, BETHEL SCHOOL OF
SUPERNATURAL MINISTRY, REDDING, CALIFORNIA

Most of us view dehydration as simply not drinking enough water. In reality dehydration, when serious enough, can lead to death. In her new book on this subject, Karen carefully and thoroughly explains what happens when we become spiritually dehydrated. Like the physical symptoms of confusion and dizziness, far too many in the body of Christ find themselves in this condition. This is a must read.

—DEANNA DUTTON
COLEAD PASTOR, WITHOUT WALLS CHURCH, MESA, ARIZONA

Hope…life…second wind…cleansing. All words I feel as I read what God has poured into Karen for this dry and discouraged generation. Karen's words are not filled with fluff or clichés but laced with grace and experience from a woman who knows what it is to need a drink from heaven. Enjoy!

—JONNA GIBSON
COLEAD PASTOR, MERCY GATE CHURCH
MOUNT BELVIEU, TEXAS

We've all faced times of spiritual thirst, times of desperately seeking the renewal only drinking from God's presence can bring. His presence brings hope and peace. His presence brings freedom and joy. Karen Schatzline's book *Dehydrated* is a must read for those of us who are thirsty.

—JINNY FORCE
MENTOR TO TEEN GIRLS AND YOUTH PASTORS' WIVES
THROUGH ASSEMBLIES OF GOD, PEN FLORIDA DISTRICT

If you have ever felt spiritually dehydrated, this book is for you. Karen does an outstanding job in presenting hope to a lost and thirsty world throughout these pages. I love the personal touches Karen puts on this book as she shares from her own experiences, her family, and her ministry. As you begin this journey, I pray you will savor each page as a good cold drink of water on a hot summer day. Let it seep into your spirit, renew and refresh you, and cause you to walk away with a new perspective of what God has in store for you.

—RESE MOORE
DIRECTOR, WEST FLORIDA DISTRICT WOMEN'S MINISTRIES

We all have become thirsty at one time or another, whether we are exercising, working, or just sitting around. Thirst can only be satisfied by hydrating our bodies. In this book Karen has so beautifully outlined ways to hydrate our lives with God our Father. We have all become dry and thirsty for the things of God but can't seem to find the right solution; Karen has given us the solutions to cure our dehydration and stay hydrated so we can be what God has called us to be. This book will challenge you like no other book you have read to grasp a hold of the things of God so you will not fall into the devil's schemes of becoming dehydrated. So give yourself a spiritual IV by reading this book. Stay hydrated, my friends.

—GARY SAPP
NATIONAL YOUTH REPRESENTATIVE, ONE CHILD MATTERS

Karen Schatzline is a forward thinker and an amazing communicator! Her new book *Dehydrated* will quench the thirst and longing of anyone wanting to grow closer to God. I highly recommend her message of inspiration and hope!

—DEBORAH PRICE HORTON
COLEAD PASTOR, BROWNSVILLE ASSEMBLY OF GOD
PENSACOLA, FLORIDA

An invigorating word infused with effervescent hope for the wasted and vacant! In this book, Karen effectively portrays the Father's desire to bring healing and refreshing waters to the broken and thirsty. These pages are infused with an effervescent hope that the "God of Encounters" is ardently waiting to pour Himself upon the despondent and vacant heart, and they effectively portray His desire to quench the thirst of the wasted and destitute of spirit.

—TIFFANY IVEY
COLEAD PASTOR, CHRIST ALIVE CHURCH
NEWTON, NORTH CAROLINA

Human beings are able to go forty days without food before damage occurs to the body, but only three days without water. Just as water is vital to our physical bodies, the water of God's Spirit is vital to our souls. We see the effects of a thirsty generation and of the Psalm 42 deer panting for water all around. I am so excited about how the new book *Dehydrated* by my friend Karen Schatzline is going to satisfy thirsty souls and refresh the dreams of a prophetic generation.

—Jay Stewart
Founding Pastor, TheRefuge.net
JayStewart.tv

I'd be hard-pressed to find a voice as pure and authentic as Karen Schatzline's; and I praise God for her obedience as a mentor to an entire generation. With *Dehydrated* she extends her refreshingly honest style to print. From beginning to end, you'll be captivated by her personal stories and life lessons, which infuse you with the hope, purpose, and passion that you so desperately crave. Truly, *Dehydrated* is a launching point for your destiny!

—Kyle Winkler
Founder, Kyle Winkler Ministries
Author, *Silence Satan*
www.kylewinkler.org

Please don't put this book down! The word that Karen Schatzline is bringing forth to all of us is desperately needed. You will experience a true encounter with your Abba Father as you drink from His fountain through *Dehydrated*. This book is going to bring life and freedom to the multitudes.

—Kristi Schatzline
Copastor, Daystar Family Church
Northport, Alabama

Karen Schatzline's book *Dehydrated* is for every person experiencing life's challenging, unpredictable, and draining effects! Karen shows us how the secret to our survival and success begins and ends with a personal wellspring of God's presence.

Her writing is reflective and empowering and will inspire every reader to initiate a passionate pursuit to drink deeply and be filled to the fullness with His living waters!

—CARMEN LETT
COPASTOR, NEW DESTINY INTERNATIONAL CHURCH
ST. PETERSBURG, FLORIDA
LIFE COACH, WHOLENESSLIFECOACH.COM

Karen has done it again! *Dehydrated* is a word that people need to grasp a hold of. This book has the power to reach in and speak life to those who have lost all hope. What a great reminder that He is only a whisper away if we will open ourselves up and be ready for an encounter with God.

—CYNDI DRAUGHON
WOMEN'S DIRECTOR, ALABAMA ASSEMBLIES OF GOD

Karen Schatzline's *Dehydrated* is a masterpiece describing the spiritual dehydration and lack of personal intimacy of the vast majority of people today, both Christian and non-Christian. It is an accurate portrayal of people letting down their "buckets" filled with problems, hurts, fears, and insecurities but failing to draw and drink the life-giving waters of Jesus, and intimacy with the Holy Spirit. *Dehydrated* is a powerful answer to the problems of inferiority, mediocrity, and weariness with life as a whole. It is written in an entertaining, easy-to-read style with many personal and life application stories by a gifted woman of God who has much experience as a wife, mother, and evangelist. I highly endorse and recommend *Dehydrated* as a source of personal and spiritual refreshment and a tool for discipleship.

—DAVID GARCIA
LEAD PASTOR, GRACE WORLD OUTREACH CHURCH
BROOKSVILLE, FLORIDA
AUTHOR, *PORTRAIT OF A POWERFUL LAST-DAY CHRISTIAN*
AND *SEX IN DATING*

Karen is a woman I greatly admire and respect. The Lord has amplified her voice in a very crucial hour of desperation to the hurting, discouraged, lost, and "dehydrated." As you read through the pages of this book you will find yourself being refreshed while being inspired. This book will guide you to the living water that is waiting for you at the well.

—MICHELLE MONTERA
EVANGELIST, MERCY SEAT MIDWEST, SPRINGFIELD, MISSOURI

"I am about to do something new. See, I have already begun! Do you not see it? I will make a pathway through the wilderness. I will create rivers in the dry wasteland" (Isa. 43:19, NLT). God's Word is our manna and the truth we stand upon. This scripture is a promise that He will do a new thing, He makes a new path, and He will create fresh water where life has become dry! Our lives are filled with pursuits and journeys that lead us at times in barren places. When we are trusting Him, He is directing our every step and sometimes it is that barren, desert place where we find Him in a way we have never known Him. Karen has beautifully and candidly taken us on her journey and allowed us to see a glimpse of what He has revealed to her. This book revives the soul and refreshes the spirit. This book, *Dehydrated*, and Karen are a gift to the Kingdom of God!

—PASTOR LEISA NELSON
THE ROCK FAMILY WORSHIP CENTER, HUNTSVILLE, ALABAMA

DEDICATION

To Pat, Abby, Nate, Adrienne, and Jackson—without you I would not have been able to write this book. I love you with all my heart.

I dedicate this book to you, Sweetheart; my best friend, husband, confidant, hero, and love of my life—Pat Schatzline. Thank you for believing in me when I didn't believe in myself, and for pushing me beyond my comfort zone to dream big dreams on our amazing adventure. Your love for God, your character, integrity, and stand for truth have given our family a deep desire to run after the heart of God. Thank you for teaching our children the love of God and showing them how to live a life of purpose for God. You have been used by God to change, transform, and lead a generation back to the heart of the Father. You are my world and truly the wind beneath my wings.

Abby, Nate, Adrienne, and Jackson, you all are truly my gifts from God. I am so proud to be your mom, friend, and biggest cheerleader. You make me want to be better and push me to be the best I can be. You have inspired me and brought more joy to my life than I could have ever dreamed of. The four of you will soar higher than Dad and I could ever imagine and will most definitely change the world. Thank you for being patient and having grace for me as I completed this project.

CONTENTS

ACKNOWLEDGMENTS

T O MY AMAZING parents, John and Gail Brown—because of your deep love and faithfulness to God, I grew up truly understanding the love of our heavenly Father. Your purity and integrity have shaped the woman I am today. You have been the voice of love and encouragement to me throughout my life. Thank you for believing in me and encouraging me to dream big dreams and pursue greatness.

To my amazing assistant and spiritual daughter, Jamie Kowalski, thank you for keeping me organized and helping me with everything during this process. You are so wonderful, and I could not have accomplished this without you.

To three women whom I consider to be spiritual mothers in my life—Carol Parritt, Tava Brice, and Phyllis Sawyer—thank you for being such godly examples of women of God to me. Your lives of love, grace, purity, and strength have so inspired me and constantly pushed me to grow closer to the Father and be a better woman in every area of my life.

To Debbie Marrie, Adrienne Gaines, Woodley Auguste, Ann Mulchan, and the entire team at Charisma Media—thank you for believing in me and in the vision of this book. I am sincerely grateful for all that you have done. You are truly a joy to work with. Your pursuit of God and desire to bring the right message and healing to the world is amazing.

To the board and ministry supporters of Remnant Ministries International—thank you for believing in the message that God has given Pat and me. We love and honor you deeply!

FOREWORD

H OW MANY TIMES do we hear the same conversation from those around us: *"I'm so tired, busy, overextended, overscheduled,"* and we too feel the same way? The demands of everyday life take a toll on our physical bodies, our mental clarity, and our relationships and leave us feeling that there is no time to stop for the refreshment we need from the Word of God and His presence.

Karen Schatzline recognizes this lack of nourishment and invites us to experience the presence of God for the first time—or again, for those who already know how powerfully the saturating atmosphere can soothe even the driest of souls.

As we have visited with Pat and Karen Schatzline over the past years, I have loved their passion to stand up for truth, to press in and invite their listeners to experience change and not just share empty words of instruction. Karen's delivery in sermons along with God's powerful anointing can bring a chorus of weeping throughout the crowd, reflecting their desire for something more from the heavenly realm.

In *Dehydrated* she addresses the story of the Samaritan woman at the well. This lady had a past and a present. Yet Jesus, the Master and Lord of all, took the time to speak to her of a water that could saturate to the point that she would never thirst again. This water gives life more abundant, no matter how far you have strayed, no matter your past, and no matter your current situation.

Wherever you are on your spiritual journey, this book is for you. Set those distracting items aside, direct your attention to the teaching and sharing of real life stories in Karen's writings, and get ready to experience the powerful presence of the Almighty.

—JONI LAMB
COFOUNDER, DAYSTAR TELEVISION NETWORK

FOREWORD

DEHYDRATED IS A word that invokes many associations. I can remember going to Hot Springs, Arkansas as a kid and playing some outdoor pickup basketball. Being from Northern California, I wasn't ready for the heat combined with the Jurassic Park humidity of the Deep South. While playing I was sweating and beginning to hyperventilate, and eventually passed out. Next thing I knew my relatives were resuscitating me and pouring water in my mouth (face, nose, and Afro). I can remember how desperately thirsty I was and how unbelievably satisfying the drink was. That water fountain seemed divine, and I was preconditioned with unprecedented desperation.

Conditions prior to historic revivals have always been desperate. The graver the times the more positioned and primed people are for resuscitation and their epic "drink." History confirms that without exception, the depth of barrenness prior to a move of God is commensurate to the degree of the outpouring. Today both the world we live in and the churches we go to are equally desperate, although neither side may realize either the severity or the solution.

Karen Schatzline has released this incredible, heartfelt, written "flashpoint" that you hold in your hands. She has prophetically put her finger on the pulse of a coming move of the Spirit.

I've had the Lord say to me that He was opening the

encounter realm (making encounters with heaven more
readily available) in this season, and it would revive the
basic follower of Christ and awaken the run-of-the-mill
secular heart. *Dehydrated* hits this theme head-on and
brings personal insights, biblical truths, and practical
principles that will propel you into your encounter. I was
both spiritually inspired and infused, page after page.
Karen takes you into both the mind-set of the woman at
the well and the mind of Christ, and also connects the
dots of your journey. Her unique style of heartfelt trans-
parency and seasoned experiences takes you from your
immovable deficit to your imminent destiny.

Karen and her husband, Pat, are generals who have been
through the battles and know the private wars people are
fighting. They have laid hold of the timeless weaponry
and the eternal wisdom that will launch you into a fresh
encounter and a mighty, personal outpouring. There are
exploits awaiting the average believer and nations waiting
to be impacted by the spiritual tsunami that will be triggered by the dehydrated who found their wells. I can con-
fidently recommend this book and author to you. Get
ready for your drink!

—SEAN SMITH
@REVSEANSMITH, AUTHOR OF *I AM YOUR SIGN* AND
PROPHETIC EVANGELISM
WWW.SEANSMITHMINISTRIES.COM

INTRODUCTION

I HAVE TRAVELED ACROSS the world speaking a message of hope and restoration, and the statement that I hear over and over again is this: "I'm so dry and exhausted. There has got to be more to this life that I am living."

There is a cry coming from the throne of God for an awakening to take place in this generation. The busyness and struggle of everyday life can not only exhaust us but also strain our relationship with God! One morning God spoke to my heart and said that the best word to describe how most of us feel is *dehydrated*!

"We are so thirsty!" Those are the words my family echoed late one afternoon after we had finished a long hike into the mountains. In our carelessness we had not carried enough water for our journey. Luckily we made it out of the woods to the water bottle waiting for us in our car, which was parked at the end of the hiking trail.

Have you ever felt that way—dry, thirsty, and desperate for refreshment? I have learned that, too often, you don't even realize you're thirsty or dehydrated until it's too late in your journey. By that time it has taken a toll on your body, both physically and mentally, and your body screams for refreshment.

The same is true of the life journey. So many people are thirsty and desperately seeking relief for the issues that have left them empty, parched, and exhausted. They are desperately seeking answers!

Life has a way of depleting our spiritual "wells." It's time to head back to the well to get refilled. The Bible is filled with the answers we need. In the story of a woman Jesus met at Jacob's well, the Bible talks about our desperation and thirst, and provides the relief we are seeking.

In John 4:10 Jesus told the woman, "If you knew the generosity of God and who I am, you would be asking me for a drink, and I would give you fresh, living water" (THE MESSAGE).

So very often, we go to the well out of desperation. With our buckets in hand, we present our cases to God. We pour out everything to Him, dumping our guilt, shame, fears, concerns, insecurities, anxiety, and sins. Rarely, however, do we drink of the life-giving water He wants to provide. That water would keep us refreshed and free from spiritual dehydration; but instead, we walk away still dry and thirsty, without receiving the living water He offers freely.

THE "WELL EXPERIENCE"

As a young girl I was lonely, insecure, and hopelessly searching for identity and purpose. One hot, muggy, Florida morning, while sitting alone on a concrete bench in the middle of the school courtyard, I began a journey that would change the course of my life forever. There on that bench, I learned to hear the voice of God as He sat beside me and talked with me.

This is the place where Jesus sits, on the well of Jacob (the deceiver), so that we can see truth clearly and live in continual freedom and joy and peace. That is where I found Him that day, on a concrete bench that became my personal "well experience" with Jesus. Throughout my ensuing years as a wife, mom, pastor's wife, and evangelist, I have had many more encounters that have led me to taste the living water. Those encounters have changed me from a dry and barren land to a fountain that is able to pour out and lead others to their own well experiences with the Savior.

There is a well experience for everyone. It's that moment when Jesus sits down to talk with you alone. The Bible says that Jesus sat down at Jacob's well (John 4:6). In doing so He set the stage for a supernatural encounter with God. The power of the encounter! It is the moment when Jesus silences the voice of the deceiver (the enemy) in your life. It is a divine appointment, a specific time when God "shows up" on your behalf. The moment is marked by His presence, power, and deliverance. It is a realization that change has been waiting on you, and there *is* more available than what you have settled for in your life so far.

This message is for those who long to walk to the front and worship in God's presence but feel that the guilt and shame of the past get in their way and keep them chained to their seats. It is for those who feel they don't matter or don't deserve to have a real relationship with a loving, caring, healing Savior—those who have become too tired, overwhelmed, and dry to fight the enemy.

God is waiting on you. In the middle of your desert, in a life that might feel like a wasteland, He has streams of refreshing, life-giving water. All you have to do is show up and drink, and you will never thirst again.

Our physical bodies can go without water for only three days before they start shutting down. At that point we become unable to function as we were created to, and our minds start playing tricks on us. In the same way, when we aren't regularly filled up spiritually, we are unable to function properly as Christians. Because of spiritual dehydration, our hope deteriorates, we lose focus, and we become ineffective in life.

As you take this journey with me, I challenge you to

open yourself up to the God encounters, the well experiences that will change you from the inside out. In them, you'll be transformed for a lifetime, not just a moment.

No matter where you come from or what is in your past, God still wants to spend time with you, so take these words to heart:

> Forget all that [is behind you]—it is nothing compared to what I am going to do. For I am about to do something new. See, I have already begun! Do you not see it? I will make a pathway through the wilderness. I will create rivers in the dry wasteland.
> —ISAIAH 43:18–19, NLT

He wants to set you free and give you a fresh start. He issues second chances upon request. It's time for you to realize that your life matters and that God loves you and has a purpose for your life. You're not here by chance. He is waiting to have a personal relationship in which He walks with you and talks with you and leads you on an amazing adventure full of life and joy and peace and fulfillment.

Buckle up, because this journey will force you to challenge everything you thought was normal in your weary life. God uses the dirty, messed up, forgotten nobodies; He heals and sets them free and uses them to clean up this messy world. It happened to the woman at the well. She didn't deserve the kindness Jesus gave her, but He decided that she was worth His time. God had bigger plans for her than she had for herself—and not just for her, but also for those she would encounter.

As you embark on this journey let me ask you: Does God know where you are today? Does He know your circumstances, issues, and struggles? The answer is *absolutely*! He knows, and He is preparing an encounter just for you and Him to have a conversation about that plan for your life. He has called you to rise up! If you will allow Him, He will walk you through a journey to find freedom, joy, fulfillment, and purpose as you read these pages.

Your journey is both temporal and eternal. There will come a day when you and I will hear these words: "The Spirit and the bride say, 'Come!' And let the one who hears say, 'Come!' Let the one who is thirsty come; and let the one who wishes take the free gift of the water of life" (Rev. 22:17).

He is waiting to meet with you. Are you thirsty today? Are you dehydrated by the world and the issues of life? Will you come and drink?

Chapter 1

CONVERSATIONS
WITH THE KING

*I do not consider myself yet to have taken hold
of it. But one thing I do: Forgetting what is
behind and straining toward what is ahead...*
—PHILIPPIANS 3:13

HAVE YOU EVER sat in a crowd of hundreds of
people and felt completely and utterly alone,
isolated, unseen by those around you, and imprisoned
by fear and insecurities? Have you ever felt as if you were
drowning, but you were the only one able to hear your
screams? Have you ever been so dry and thirsty for life
that relief from your pain seemed like an ongoing mirage
in your desert of lost hope?

Well, get ready, because God has an encounter waiting
for you today. He promises rivers in your desert. This
familiar but reworded passage will encourage you:

> Do not remember the things that have happened
> before. Do not think about the things of the past.
> See, I will do a new thing. It will begin happening
> now. Will you not know about it? I will even make a
> road in the wilderness, and rivers in the desert.
> —ISAIAH 43:18–19, NLV

As a young girl I was held hostage to my own fear and
insecurities. But praise God! He rescued me. I will share
more about that soon, but right now as you are reading, I

believe there will be moments when you have to put down the book and crawl into your prayer closet to encounter the loving Father God who desires to know and heal and refresh you. I believe there will be moments of awakening when the Holy Spirit walks into your room and saturates your life with healing oil.

So get ready! This adventure will lead you to freedom.

There is such a stirring in my heart for you to realize that you are not alone! God is calling you out of your comfort zone and out of the familiar. Some of you have been hiding for too long; Jesus is giving you permission to step out of the darkness into the marvelous light today. Step out of the shadows of the past and step forward with boldness and strength as you are washed in the presence of God. *He wants to have intentional encounters with you*! He wants to meet you where you are and breathe new life into you.

I'll never forget one morning when I went down to our basement, as I often do, to work out and get my brain functioning so I could take on the day. My brain does not function well until I work out. And there are no goals or visions for the day until I do. While I occasionally drink coffee, the adrenaline of torturing my body through a strenuous workout is my morning drug of choice. It jolts my mind and body into submission and keeps them from rebelling throughout the day.

As I prepared and procrastinated on this particular morning, I shoved our coffee table out of the way and popped in my workout CD. When I did, my devotional book fell off the table. As I picked it up I felt a slight pull to read that day's devotions, but I pushed past it and went straight to my workout. After all, my body needed to get it going!

Taking care of our bodies is important, so I try to eat right and drink plenty of water. But sometimes it's not our physical bodies that are thirsty; it is our spirits. The Bible describes this thirst: "You, God, are my God, earnestly I seek you; I thirst for you, my whole being longs for you, in a dry and parched land where there is no water" (Ps. 63:1).

As I exercised and worked up a thirst, I reached for my water bottle and knocked over the devotional again. Slightly frustrated, I shoved it to the side. As I continued working out, I bumped into the coffee table yet again and knocked over the devotional one more time. I might not be the most coordinated person around, but in that moment I heard the Holy Spirit speak to my heart. He said, "Karen, I desire intentional encounters with you. I don't want random, accidental encounters, but rather intentional ones."

Often, we are so busy with so many things that God is the last thing on our list. We know all too well that the last item on the list rarely gets done. He has to be at the top of the list! It's time for us to slow down, take a deep breath, and make our relationship with God our top priority.

Matthew 5:6 says: "Blessed are those who hunger and thirst for righteousness, for they will be filled." It occurred to me in that moment, that while I had gone to great lengths to strengthen and prepare my physical body, I had neglected my spirit. I sensed God telling me that if I would spend even half the time caring for my spirit—entering into His presence, pursuing Him, and desiring Him—that I do caring for and nurturing my flesh, my day would be far different from normal. If I would purposely run after Him, I would be filled with joy and passion and freedom to take on the day and whatever the enemy threw at me. In that pursuit of God, I would find my strength.

Needless to say, I stopped the workout, opened my devotional, and strengthened my spirit for the day ahead.

THE INVITING, RESTORING GOD

I thank God that He is a loving Father who nudges us and draws us into His presence. There are times where we become too preoccupied with the pain of our lives to notice Jesus standing right in front of us. We don't realize He is there with outstretched arms and a great big bucket full of life-giving water for us.

It's time for your encounter *today*. A certain Bible account speaks to such encounters, and I have been waiting to share it with you. It rejuvenates my spirit every time I read it. But first let me set the stage: It was hot outside and Jesus's disciples went to buy lunch. Meanwhile, Jesus sat by a well. He had nothing with which to scoop out the cool water, although that was not really why He was there. He was there because a certain woman needed a personal encounter with the Messiah! She wasn't worthy, in man's opinion, to have an encounter with the Savior. She was a Samaritan and was therefore considered by the Jews to be no better than a dog. She was dirty, not someone a Jew wanted to be seen with. What kind of God would talk to a woman like that? Just one—His name is Jesus!

Now for the passage that I absolutely love. Go ahead! Soak in these words of hope, healing, and freedom:

> A woman, a Samaritan, came to draw water. Jesus said, "Would you give me a drink of water?" (His disciples had gone to the village to buy food for lunch.) The Samaritan woman, taken aback, asked, "How come you, a Jew, are asking me, a Samaritan woman, for a drink?" (Jews in those days wouldn't be caught dead talking to Samaritans.)
> —JOHN 4:7–9, THE MESSAGE

I imagine the woman was startled to find Jesus sitting there. She didn't know who He was or why He was there at that time of day. I would almost bet that she felt ashamed and kept her head down, afraid to look Him in the eyes, fearing they would not be eyes of compassion or acceptance.

Have you ever felt like you were unworthy to hear Jesus talk to you, unworthy even to enter into His presence? Is there a sense that you have been through too much or that too much has been done to you for such an encounter to happen?

Let me tell you: Jesus has decided that you are worth His time! You are valued. You are important. You are not an "oops" or an accident, but a child of the King. Your life matters!

This Samaritan woman had been used, abused, and thrown away more than once. People proudly declared her dirty. After all, she had already been through five husbands, and the man she was living with was not her husband. In those days (and even today in much of the Middle East) if you committed adultery, you were stoned to death. She was obviously still alive, but really she was dead inside. She had been rejected by five different men, most likely because she had not given them a child. Being unable to produce a child was seen as a curse in those days. In First Samuel chapter 1, Hannah cried out for a child to give her husband, Elkanah. Sarah, the wife of Abraham longed to give birth to a son for her husband. Not giving a child to your husband was considered shameful.

The Samaritan woman had five husbands—*five* being the number of grace.[1] Do you see? Her grace had run out. She was at her end! She had nothing left, so she decided to do it in her own strength and take matters into her own hands.

Don't we all do that at times? The grace has run out, so in desperation we take action. The Samaritan woman did just that and was now living with the sixth man. The

number six is the number for humankind and the sinful
nature.[2] She had given up on grace and took matters into
her own hands. She decided: "If this doesn't work out, I'll
just move on to the next thing."

She was settling for second best in her life, accepting
leftovers instead of waiting on the blessings of God. Her
choices left her empty, but on this particular day the seventh Man would enter her life! She would meet Jesus,
the only one who could satisfy her deepest longing and
quench the thirst of her spirit. Jesus, the seventh Man—
with seven being the representation of spiritual perfection
and resurrection![3]

Are you getting this? When the grace ran out, she ran
to man for answers and tried everything she knew to do in
her own strength. She was at the end of herself. In a sense,
it was a spiritual death. That was when she came upon the
seventh Man, who would give her a second chance at life.
Only He could resurrect her dry and weary soul. Only He
could bring her life and make her whole again.

THE GREAT PHYSICIAN IS IN

You may have been used, discarded, and abandoned. The
world may have called you dirty, rejected, jobless, divorced,
broke, and worthless. God doesn't call you by the world's
labels. God calls you His child! It's time to discard the
pain and shame of your yesterday in order to see clearly
what God has for your future! It's time to stop trying to do
things in your own strength and instead relinquish control to God. Change has been waiting on you. Let Him
resurrect you!

The Samaritan woman was all alone. She went to draw
water at noon when everyone else was home resting. Her
head was hung low. She looked at no one. For God to truly

change and use her, she had to first have a one-on-one encounter with the Savior.

The same is true for us. The encounter comes the moment we allow God to open our hearts and do surgery to repair us. I have learned this concept firsthand. Over the past several years I have had my share of surgeries, ranging from a discectomy for a ruptured disc in my neck, to having a hysterectomy because of many years of painful issues. Those issues would be the reason my husband, Pat, and I could not conceive after the birth of our son, Nate. (Little did I know that what I called an *issue*, God called a *miracle*, as I will explain soon.)

My prayer is that you have an appointment with the Great Physician today. There is nothing better! I have never entered His throne room without leaving completely transformed. As important as it is to consult medical doctors at times, meetings with the Great Physician are much better. It amazes me that when I visit a doctor and explain exactly where it hurts, he or she proceeds to press, prod, and poke that exact spot. I want to say, "Really? Did you not just hear me say that it hurts?"

Many times, this is the reason we don't enter the Great Physician's presence—because we pour out our heart and cry and wail and tell God exactly what's wrong and about all the pain we feel. Then He administers pressure to areas of our lives that lay hidden below the surface. He does this to isolate the root cause of our pain.

It's not comfortable or pleasant to face the realities of our issues. But in order to receive healing, we need a clear understanding of the problem. It's time we stopped self-medicating, numbing, and covering up our pain, and started dealing with it head-on. Every pain has a root; usually it is based in fear, insecurity, hurts, bitterness, and anger. God wants to heal us, not just conceal our wounds or allow them to fester. His healing water will bring wholeness to the very root of our pain!

This is what happened to the Samaritan woman. Change arrived in the form of a Savior. The same Savior wants to interact with us:

> So here's what I want you to do, God helping you: Take your everyday, ordinary life—your sleeping, eating, going-to-work, and walking-around life— and place it before God as an offering. Embracing what God does for you is the best thing you can do for him. Don't become so well-adjusted to your culture that you fit into it without even thinking. Instead, fix your attention on God. You'll be changed from the inside out. Readily recognize what he wants from you, and quickly respond to it. Unlike the culture around you, always dragging you down to its level of immaturity, God brings the best out of you, develops well-formed maturity in you.
> —ROMANS 12:1–2, THE MESSAGE

Like the woman at the well, you need to be changed from the *inside*. God is calling you to something new, something so real and powerful that it dramatically changes you. It's time to change your clothes; change your wineskin; change the name you were once known by in society.

BREAK OPEN YOUR COCOON

When I think of change, I think of the butterfly. My twelve-year-old daughter, Abby, and I absolutely love the butterfly exhibit at the zoo. Every year we go through the same routine: We cannot wait for the exhibit to open, and when it does, we rush to the zoo and head straight for the butterflies. We enter the exhibit filled with excitement and wonder, wanting so badly for a butterfly to land on us.

Usually it takes just a few minutes until a butterfly gracefully perches on Abby's shoulder. Then, in a fraction of a moment, excitement turns to panic when the butterfly won't let go. Our year-long wait ends in a very special moment lasting all of five minutes, and Abby can't wait to leave the exhibit. As soon as we are safely out, she exclaims, "I can't wait for next year!"

I think the reason we love butterflies so much is because of the process they endure to become what they were meant to be. Each butterfly has to go through a series of intense changes known as *metamorphosis*. It is a Greek word meaning "the process of transformation from an immature form to an adult form in two or more distinct stages."[4] It also means "a change of the form or nature of a thing or person into a completely different one by natural or supernatural means."[5]

Are you getting this? It's the grow-up process! We love the butterfly because it represents us. It has to go from an egg, to a larva, to a nasty little caterpillar, to a cocoon before it ever becomes the beautiful butterfly we admire in awe and wonder. The butterfly faces many challenges and struggles along its journey to greatness and beauty. Every stage is important to its growth and purpose.

One of the problems I see as I travel the nation is that many people give up too early in their journey. They cannot see past the worm they perceive themselves to be. They get stuck crawling around and grabbing whatever they can in order to survive. Then they assume that what they found must be all there is. But they are wrong; there is a beautiful butterfly on the way, just waiting to break free.

Here's the key: in order to reach the point of freedom, we have to leave the past behind and allow ourselves to be transformed. We have to leave the hurt, offenses, guilt, shame, and failures in the rearview mirror, along with our crutches and excuses. Then we can enter the cocoon with God. (Pardon my mixing of metaphors, but we are also like photographs waiting to be developed; we must enter the darkroom in order to be developed.)

What we often fail to realize is that, although the chrysalis (or cocoon) stage of our lives seems dark and lonely, the word means "protected stage of development."[6] You see, God draws us into what seems like a dark, isolated season of life; but really it is a time of protected development during which we are alone with Him—our audience of one!

More times than not, we get stuck in the cocoon phase because we think it is just too hard to dig our way out of the past. We are unwilling to fight. Can I tell you something? God is not only calling us to the waters of refreshing; He is also calling us to fight and put the devil back where he belongs—under our feet!

We *must* learn to fight. My daughter, Abby, always wants to help the struggling butterfly leave its cocoon. Once, in our backyard, we saw a cocoon on our window. The butterfly was struggling to get out. It was a beautiful sight. Abby said, "Mommy, help it! Can't you help it get out of the cocoon?"

Quickly I told her that I could, but I wouldn't. This upset Abby, and she stressed to me that the butterfly needed my help. I explained that I could not help the butterfly, because if I did, I would actually harm it.

You see, helping the butterfly open its cocoon interrupts its journey at a critical stage. It would stretch out its beautiful wings and fly high in the sky. However, in just moments it would fall to the ground and perish. As I explained to Abby, during the butterfly's struggle to get free, its blood is pumped through its wings, giving it the strength to fly.

Abby understood. So we stood and watched the butterfly gain its strength. When it broke free, it flew vigorously across the backyard in all its splendor. That day I was able to teach my daughter the valuable lesson that in our struggles we become strong. She has faced struggles in her young life. I want her always to know that struggles should not make her bitter, angry, hurt, or wounded; they should make her stronger.

That is what the struggles in my life have done. They have made me stronger! The dry, dehydrated times in my life have caused me to search out the living water that God has to offer. I have learned to stop complaining and start becoming part of the solution!

HIDING, IN PLAIN SIGHT

Sometimes in the process of change, we need help. Jesus wants to help us! Look at what Scripture says He will do:

> So, friends, take a firm stand, feet on the ground and head high. Keep a tight grip on what you were taught, whether in personal conversation or by our letter. May Jesus himself and God our Father, who reached out in love and surprised you with gifts of unending help and confidence, put a fresh heart in you, invigorate your work, enliven your speech.
> —2 THESSALONIANS 2:15–17, THE MESSAGE

God is calling you and asking, "Can I have a minute of your time?" I believe that as you are reading, He is about to sit down beside you because He wants to talk to you. If He interrupted a Samaritan woman, He will surely interrupt you! He wants to invade the room you are in right now. Let Him do it. The answers you seek can only be found in His presence. Turn off the computer and the TV. Forget about Instagram, Twitter, and Facebook. Put down your phone, and He will speak to you!

The problem is that we get so busy throughout the day

that we rarely make time to just sit and hear what God has to say. That is our loss, because when He comes near, *it is amazing*! He turns our thinking inside out. The woman at the well was a Samaritan, yet Jesus asked her for a drink. Even more amazing is the fact that in giving Him a drink, her thirst was quenched!

Look at the passage again:

> Jesus answered, "If you knew the generosity of God and who I am, you would be asking me for a drink, and I would give you fresh, living water." The woman said, "Sir, you don't even have a bucket to draw with, and this well is deep. So how are you going to get this 'living water'? Are you a better man than our ancestor Jacob, who dug this well and drank from it, he and his sons and livestock, and passed it down to us?" Jesus said, "Everyone who drinks this water will get thirsty again and again. Anyone who drinks the water I give will never thirst—not ever. The water I give will be an artesian spring within, gushing fountains of endless life." The woman said, "Sir, give me this water so I won't ever get thirsty, won't ever have to come back to this well again!"
> —JOHN 4:10–15, THE MESSAGE

Wow! Can you see how she went from shame and despair to desiring what He offered? Her eyes were opened. He was telling her, "While you tried everything under the sun, it left you empty and wanting; but I will satisfy your deepest needs and longings. Everything else just pacifies!" This broken woman went to the well at the hottest time of day just to avoid the crowd, the ridicule, and the rejection. She wished she didn't have to go back there, not because she was lazy or procrastinating, but because the well was a constant reminder of her low status in society. She waited and risked the brutal heat of the day hoping to avoid the sneers, the whispering behind her back, the rejection from *everyone*.

The well was an everyday reminder of the Samaritan woman's failure, and she was at her end. The most safety she could find was to go there at noon when the naysayers and mockers were sitting at home in the shade.

THE DECEIVER'S WELL

Remember that this was the well Jacob gave to Joseph. It was in Sychar, which was also known as Shechem, the city in which Jacob also built an altar.

In Genesis chapters 25 and 27, Jacob was known as a deceiver. Then, in Genesis 32, he wrestled with God. He walked away from that place with a limp, a sign of brokenness. There in Peniel, Jacob's name was changed to Israel, because he had wrestled with God and man and had overcome (Gen. 32:28).

Years later, Jacob's son, Joseph, experienced great rejection from his jealous brothers. Shechem is the place where Joseph's brothers were thought to be when Jacob sent him to find them. Many believe that Shechem is where Joseph's brothers sold him into slavery and also where his bones were eventually buried.

Jacob gave Joseph that land. Therefore, the well symbolizes a place of deception and rejection. But Joseph's life did not end in rejection. Although he was bitterly betrayed, entrapped, and scorned, people ultimately bowed before him. Amazingly, his life reflects that of Jesus: Joseph wore a coat of many colors (representing all nations); he was thrown in the pit (representing death); he was later treated as a king (as was Jesus on Palm Sunday); and he was restored to the palace (a parallel of Christ's ascension).

Centuries later, the Samaritan woman went to the same place of deception and rejection. Deceived by the enemy and rejected by men, women, and Jews,[7] and wanting to be alone with her sorrow, she went to the well at noon. But she would not be alone that day. Instead, she would meet a Man who sat on the well of deceit so that her eyes could be opened to the truth of who she was meant to be. At that well, she would meet the Man of sorrows.

Why is Jesus known by this name? Isaiah prophesied it and related it to the ultimate sacrifice Jesus made on our behalf:

> He was despised and rejected—a man of sorrows, acquainted with deepest grief. We turned our backs on him and looked the other way. He was despised, and we did not care. Yet it was our weaknesses he carried; it was our sorrows that weighed him down. And we thought his troubles were a punishment from God, a punishment for his own sins! But he was pierced for our rebellion, crushed for our sins. He was beaten so we could be whole. He was whipped so we could be healed. All of us, like sheep, have strayed away. We have left God's paths to follow our own. Yet the LORD laid on him the sins of us all.
> —ISAIAH 53:3–6, NLT

At the well the deceived and rejected woman met the most rejected of all men, the Man of sorrows, Jesus! He knew her pain and decided He would not leave her there in it. He exposed the truth about her past and her history. He offered her the living water, freedom from her pain, and a life full of purpose.

During their encounter, Jesus made several challenging statements:

> It's who you are and the way you live that count before God. Your worship must engage your spirit in the pursuit of truth. That's the kind of people the

Father is out looking for: those who are simply and
honestly themselves before him in their worship.
God is sheer being itself—Spirit. Those who worship
him must do it out of their very being, their spirits,
their true selves, in adoration.
—JOHN 4:23–24, THE MESSAGE

Still unsure of Him, the Samaritan woman said, "I don't
know about that. I do know that the Messiah is coming.
When he arrives, we'll get the whole story" (John 4:25,
THE MESSAGE).

Then Jesus told her who He was! "'I am he,' said Jesus.
'You don't have to wait any longer or look any further"
(John 4:26, THE MESSAGE).

In essence, He said, "Stop searching! I'm right here,
calling your name." (As you read these words, I want you
to know that He is right there with *you*, calling *you* into
His presence!)

Jesus convinced the Samaritan woman that He was
the living water. He healed her and gave her a future. I
love what happens next. Once her eyes were opened, she
dropped her watering pot and ran back to tell the people
in her town about the Man at the well!

The woman took the hint and left. In her confusion
she left her water pot. Back in the village she told
the people, "Come see a man who knew all about
the things I did, who knows me inside and out. Do
you think this could be the Messiah?" And they
went out to see for themselves.
—JOHN 4:28–30, THE MESSAGE

She brought the whole city to meet Jesus! Her secret
encounter changed not only her, but everyone in town. The
same thing happens today: the time you spend with God in
private will determine the influence you have in public.

MY FIRST TRIP TO THE WELL

Like the Samaritan woman, I had a well experience that established my journey to freedom and purpose. I've already mentioned briefly what happened when I was thirteen and entering the seventh grade. I was a very timid, insecure, and fearful young girl. Growing up, my family was amazing; yet I dealt with strong feelings of being worthless and lost. At times I felt invisible, as though no one saw me or knew who I was. I was so shy that it was difficult to look people in the face or speak in public. The thought of standing in front of a crowd would make me sick or, worse, bring me to tears.

There I was, a sad little girl on her first day of seventh grade. Looking back it's almost humorous, but at the time, it was unbearable and even crippling. As I got ready for school that morning, I thought of every possible way to avoid leaving the house and facing my anxieties. Nothing seemed to work, however, so, off to the bus stop I went. I was so nervous that my hands and feet were wet with perspiration. The incredibly hot and muggy Florida weather was no help!

Leaving the comfort of elementary school and being shipped off to the seventh grade was a scary thought. In Florida seventh grade was a school all by itself, separated from all other grades as though no one knew what to do with our newly hormonal and changing young bodies. So we went off to a school all our own and prepared for integration with the middle grades.

As our bus pulled up to the school, I recognized very few people. I had friends in the sixth grade, but now sixth-graders from many schools were being dumped into one giant facility that resembled a prison. There was barbed wire around the top of the fence and people monitoring everything. All I could think of was, "What did we do to deserve such punishment?" It's crazy how the pre-teen mind works!

When I got off the bus I only had one goal in mind: to survive. For a moment I scanned the area, hoping to spot someone I knew. Of course, I didn't. I was terrified of being picked on, bullied, or just embarrassed. So I walked as quickly as I could to the far side of the courtyard in which we were to stay until the bell rang. I chose the spot farthest away from everyone.

Everyone else seemed to be laughing and talking together. Have you ever felt completely isolated and alone, even in the midst of a crowd? That is the number one goal of the enemy—to isolate you so he can attack at your most vulnerable moments.

That's where I was, so crippled by my insecurities that I pretended to look through my books so as not to seem so awkward. Sitting there, I became increasingly overwhelmed by hopelessness and loneliness and felt the nearly uncontrollable urge to cry. But I knew that if I did cry, it would mark me for the rest of the year. So I did everything I could to hold back my tears.

Just as the first tear welled up, I felt a tap on my shoulder. I jerked around to see who it was, but there was no one there. I thought to myself, "I knew it! I'm going to be bullied on the first day of prison. (I mean, seventh grade.)"

I hoped that if I ignored the tap, whoever it was would lose interest. So I went back to looking at my books. But again, I felt a tap on my shoulder and quickly turned around, hoping to catch the culprit. Once again, I saw no one. This time, however, a profound peace filled my heart, and I knew there was no *human* there.

As a thirteen-year-old girl I experienced the all-consuming presence of God as He sat next to me on that hot concrete bench in the school courtyard. Jesus met me in the midst of my fear and anxiety and hopelessness that day. I felt God's arm wrap around me and comfort me in that moment when I was so overwhelmed. It was the first time I can recall hearing the voice of God, and this is what He said to me: "Karen, I know you! I see you. You're not alone. I am here with you, and if you will allow Me to, I will walk this journey with you. You don't have to walk alone; I will always be with you!"

The God of the universe thought the pitiful, shy, insecure little girl on the bench was important enough for Him to stop and take notice of her! Shortly after that, the bell rang, and I felt different. I was invigorated, strengthened, and sensed new life in me. A new courage was building inside me. It would continue to grow all through middle and high school.

I would love to say that I immediately became bold and the life of the party or the captain of the cheering squad or the president of the debate team. But no, I stayed shy and awkward for many, many years. The difference, however, was that I knew I wasn't alone. I knew there was a bigger plan than what I could see. I knew that no matter what I faced—and I faced many challenges—God was always with me and would never leave me. In the times of temptation faced by all teenagers, I would remember that courtyard bench and the One who rescued me that day. The moment so transformed me that I would become incredibly strong-willed and purposeful in all that I did.

At times when I'm about to step out onstage to speak about hope and freedom, I look back at that little girl and am so thankful for her! I'll never forget that when she thought she was stepping into a seventh-grade prison, she was actually entering the year of her prison break! It wasn't easy, but it was worth it. I'm thankful for the struggles she plowed through and the battles she fought. Without them

I might never have found my strength or learned to recognize and hear the voice of God. I would never have known the freedom that comes from fully trusting Him. I would never have found the life-giving water that only He can give to quench my thirst and save my soul!

HE HAS ALWAYS KNOWN YOU

In your journey and your search for refreshing, God wants you to know that He knew you before you knew Him. He created you! It is just as the Samaritan woman learned: He knows everything about you—the good, the bad, and the ugly—and still He chooses to love you! God knew you before anyone else did. He was writing the scrolls of your life long before you ever knew Him.

One evening, when our daughter Abby was about four years old, she ran to me in the living room and said, "Can I tell you something, Mommy?"

I stopped what I was doing and said, "Sure, sweetheart."

She said, "I had a dream last night. You want to know what it was about?"

Of course I wanted to know, especially since she seemed so excited about it. Abby is from China. We adopted her when she was just nine months old. She truly is a gift from God, and she brings great joy to our lives. We have always been open about her adoption and are extremely grateful and blessed at how God chose to grow our family.

That evening, Abby looked at me intently and said, "Jesus came to see me in my dream last night."

Now I was intrigued and sitting on the edge of the seat as she told me what Jesus said to her: "Remember when you were in the orphanage, Abby, and I used to tell you that your mommy was coming to get you? Well, I told you and, see, she came to get you! And she loves you."

Abby said, "Isn't that neat, Mommy?" and ran back out of the room as if it were no big deal!

I sat there in a pool of tears and thanked God for knowing, loving, and visiting my daughter before I even knew her. He knew her long before we did and was orchestrating her life and planning her future. He has great plans for Abby. Even when she was just four years old He reminded her to never forget that He loves her, He knew her first, and He would never leave her.

The following passage captures the Father's love so well:

> Oh yes, you shaped me first inside, then out; you formed me in my mother's womb. I thank you, High God—you're breathtaking! Body and soul, I am marvelously made! I worship in adoration—what a creation! You know me inside and out, you know every bone in my body; you know exactly how I was made, bit by bit, how I was sculpted from nothing into something. Like an open book, you watched me grow from conception to birth; all the stages of my life were spread out before you, the days of my life all prepared before I'd even lived one day.
> —PSALM 139:13–16, THE MESSAGE

God knew you first. He also wants you to know that He is more than enough for you! Things and stuff and people cannot bring you joy or peace or freedom. Our family was not well off as I was growing up, and we may not have had all the new things some families had; but that was OK. Although I didn't fully realize it then, we had something better. My parents started the legacy of a family in covenant with God. In fact, all I really knew throughout my life was that God was right there with me. He was walking my journey with me and had a bigger plan for my life.

I realized at a young age that my current circumstances do not dictate my destiny. Your circumstances don't dictate yours, either. It's time to face off with the enemy and declare that God is enough! He is all you need. You are a warrior, a force to be reckoned with. Through and with God, you can do anything!

Are you thirsty for Him? Psalm 42:2 says: "My soul thirsts for God, for the living God. When can I go and meet with God?" What is holding you back from your encounter with Him today? What is keeping you from having a conversation with the King? There is a well before you; Jesus is sitting there waiting for you. Will you go to Him? He is calling out to you, inviting you to come as you are. He welcomes the dehydrated and thirsty to come, receive, and never thirst again.

During His encounter with the Samaritan woman, Jesus showed that He knew who she was and who He would cause her to become. God sees you in your dry place. He sees you in your pain. You are not worthless, not just another body taking up space. God values you and has plans for you. The things you have done and have been through don't lessen your value to God. He created you *and He likes what He made.* Even so, He won't leave you where He finds you; He will pull you out and take you somewhere new. He will walk you into a great adventure!

The following Scripture passage shows what a beautiful adventure it is:

> Some of you wandered for years in the desert, looking but not finding a good place to lie, half-starved and parched with thirst, staggering and stumbling, on the brink of exhaustion. Then, in your desperate condition, you called out to GOD. He got you out in the nick of time; he put your feet on a wonderful road that took you straight to a good place to live. So thank GOD for his marvelous love, for his miracle mercy to the children he loves.

He poured great draughts of water down parched
throats; the starved and hungry got plenty to eat.
—PSALM 107:4–9, THE MESSAGE

A MOMENT AT THE WELL

There is something so amazing about waking up and realizing that God loves you! He wants to invade your world.
He wants to talk with you today. He wants to take you by
the hand and say, "Let's go on a great journey together."

Will you be so desperate for Him that you will get out
of your chair and find a secret place with Him? He knows
you're busy! You may be working in an office or at a con-
struction site. The place you are in doesn't matter. Maybe
you're like me and you have to squeeze in whatever little
moments you can find with God. You might be in the
car line picking up your children from school, or at their
soccer or football practice, or at gymnastics practice as
you read these words. As I write them, my eyes are filling
up with tears. God is urging me to tell you that no matter
where you are, you can find a place with God and drink
from the well today.

He's already at the well. Will you meet Him there? Stop
what you're doing right now and find a place to meet Him.
Pray that your life will be refreshed, restored, and renewed.
God wants to heal you so that your life will be a beacon of
hope to all who come in contact with you.

In His presence there is fullness of *joy* (Ps. 16:11).

Chapter 2

I AM UNDONE!

The doorposts and thresholds shook and the temple
was filled with smoke. "Woe to me!" I cried.
—ISAIAH 6:4–5

THERE I WAS, in the middle of the bedroom floor, weeping before the Lord. Undone! That's how I felt. Completely and totally undone in God's presence. And it was so freeing! I had gone from casually studying in preparation for a Sunday service to being on my knees, bent over, and crying out to God. Just like the woman at the well in John 4, I found myself thirsty and desperate for more! I didn't want just another service. I didn't want to fulfill a duty or "perform" a message. *I wanted more!*

I was like the Samaritan woman who came to the end and was desperate. The encounter she had with the loving Savior left her undone too. Jesus had untangled her from her past and from her humdrum, everyday life. He took her from a twisted and entrapped life to a life of freedom.

At times we get so caught up in doing what it takes to get by that we forget God's call for us to be in relationship with Him. We go through the motions of serving God, but forget that there is an actual God and Savior who desires intimacy with us. So many church services become just another spiritual ritual or social gathering, rather than a time to spend with our King and fill back up for the battle we face daily.

On the floor that afternoon I realized that my life had been more about routine and ritual than relationship and intimacy with the lover of my soul. My spirit had become dry and dehydrated due to my lack of thirst. As a nurturer, I found it was possible to give out all I had while failing to nourish my own life. My cry has since become, "God, make me what You want me to be! Don't let there be anything left when You're done with me!"

There comes a time when you finally cry out, "Woe is me!" It happens when you realize that, apart from God, there is nothing good in you (Ps. 16:2). I know I can't serve or work my way into the kingdom. I have to know the King! I want my selfish flesh to die so that God's Spirit can take over and live through me. I'm not talking about phoning it in; I'm talking about having a face-to-face encounter! The apostle Paul described it this way: "And we, who with unveiled faces all reflect the Lord's glory, are being transformed into His likeness with ever-increasing glory, which comes from the Lord, who is the Spirit" (2 Cor. 3:18).

My cry that afternoon was: "I want to be transformed! I don't want to stay the same! Less of me, God; more of You."

The question I must ask is this: "Do you look like Jesus?"

We were created in the image of God, but the world so ensnares, dehydrates, and disfigures us that it cannot recognize us as God's children.

It's time we got unwrapped!

UNWRAPPED AND UNDONE

My life theme has become: "Make me undone!" With that in mind, let's take another journey together. Really, each of our lives is a journey, a great adventure with God made up of many adventures along the way. Over time I have learned to embrace and cherish each new adventure I face. I realize that God never called me to be comfortable, just willing and ready.

That's why I love to read about Isaiah. He knew about

being uncomfortable and he understood what it means to become undone before God. Just look at this passage:

> In the year that King Uzziah died, I saw the Lord, high and exalted, seated on a throne; and the train of his robe filled the temple. Above him were seraphim, each with six wings: With two wings they covered their faces, with two they covered their feet, and with two they were flying. And they were calling to one another: "Holy, holy, holy is the LORD Almighty; the whole earth is full of his glory." At the sound of their voices the doorposts and thresholds shook and the temple was filled with smoke. "Woe to me!" I cried. "*I am ruined*! For I am a man of unclean lips, and I live among a people of unclean lips, and my eyes have seen the King, the LORD Almighty." Then one of the seraphim flew to me with a live coal in his hand, which he had taken with tongs from the altar. With it he touched my mouth and said, "See, this has touched your lips; your guilt is taken away and your sin atoned for." Then I heard the voice of the LORD saying, "Whom shall I send? And who will go for us?" And I said, "Here am I. Send me!"
>
> —ISAIAH 6:1–8

Wow! Can it be that sometime between entering the throne room door and falling on his face at God's throne Isaiah got free? In verse 5, he wrote: "I am ruined!" Some translations say, "I am undone!"

This should become every Christian's cry every single day: to be undone in God's presence. The word translated "ruined" or "undone" is the Hebrew word *damah* (dawma'). It means "to be...silent; hence, to fail or perish...to destroy...cease, be cut down (off), destroy, be brought to silence, be undone, utterly"[1] In other words, it is to be brought down to what really matters.

My goal in this chapter is to get you to the place where
you can live in a state of being undone in His presence.
This is a place where the person you used to be no longer
exists, but instead, you begin to look like Jesus. Getting to
this place is a process.

I am convinced that we all truly want an encounter
with God; but we don't want to go through the unwrap-
ping process. You see, when Isaiah entered the presence of
the Almighty God, he realized how unclean he was. It was
obvious to Isaiah that he didn't look very much like God.
The encounter forced him to declare, "Undo me, God!
Start me over! Take me back. Remove my regrets. Redeem
me. Clean me. Purify me. Make me whole, zealous, and
new again!"

Isaiah screamed at himself, "Woe is me!"

Talk about a crazy moment. You haven't really felt crazy
till you scream at yourself! It's not surprising, with such a
scene to behold. The Bible says that the angels were crying,
"Holy, holy, holy!" The threshold was bumping; the bass
was thumping; the roar of the angels was deafening.

But what brought Isaiah to the point of being undone?
I believe that, like the woman at the well, Isaiah was
confronted with himself; everything that had been
hidden in his life was brought into the light. It wasn't
pretty. It left him utterly ruined and thirsting for something more. His thirst was uncomfortable, but it positioned him for change.

Thirst pushes us past our comfort zones so we can gain
access to what we need the most. Too often, we become
so comfortable in our churches that we feel no need to
dig deeper and go further in our relationship with God.
We park in the same spot, sit in the same chairs, sing the
same songs, and enjoy our rituals. We get rattled when
anything different happens because we like familiarity.

Do you see the problem with that? While we all desire to experience the fire of God, we don't necessarily want to push, plow, and dig for it. I am convinced today more than ever that we don't need a nice little visitation from the Holy Spirit. Rather, we must have a habitation! We need a "Move in with me, God" moment. That's the moment in which we say, "I'm committed to You, God. Live with me; reside in my home, my life, my family, my marriage, and my dreams."

We don't need a cozy, comfortable, feel-good fire, but *an all-consuming fire.* We've made church so soothing that people are falling asleep in God's presence, and there is no change. It is an experience, but it bears no resemblance to what Isaiah experienced in God's presence.

A Balanced "Diet"

My focus in this chapter is not on the angels that were crying, "Holy!" My focus is not on the beauty and splendor of the throne room. It's not even on the shaking of the doorposts and threshold. My focus is on Isaiah.

Have you ever felt out of place in a church service? Have you ever stood in worship, listening to the shouts of the worshippers, feeling the beating of the bass drum, watching the twirling of the banners and the jumping of the excited crowd, and somehow felt that there had to be more. Did you get the feeling that if you stopped everything and just listened and waited, God would surely speak to you?

Don't get me wrong, I love the excitement, energy, and passion of praise and worship. God loves it! But sometimes, I just want to hear the Father's voice. I'll never forget a certain service in which my husband, Pat, was going to preach. It was just *that* amazing! As the worship went crazy and I closed my eyes, God showed me a vision of a flood rushing into the building. The flood waters rose quickly and consumed everyone in inside, yet no one was alarmed and everyone continued to worship. There was such freedom in their sense of abandon.

Here's what God showed me: He wants to flood our churches and our lives with life-giving water from heaven, but we must come to the end of ourselves to find the beginning of Him! God is calling His bride back to secret encounters and passionate glances. God is calling us to cry out as David did when he said, "God—you're my God! I can't get enough of you! I've worked up such hunger and thirst for God, traveling across dry and weary deserts" (Ps. 63:1, THE MESSAGE).

The problem is that too many of us are on spiritual diets. We're starving ourselves of the nutrients needed for a healthy relationship with God. Then we get so hungry and thirsty that we go on spiritual binges. As a result, our lives are unbalanced. This cycle of extremes leaves us weak and ill-prepared for the journey ahead. Unless we maintain an intimate devotional life, we will surely experience emotional lives. We need to constantly feed on the Word of God—every day. This in turn makes us crave for more and more of His Word as our spirits become strengthened by it.

What would happen if, instead of fulfilling our obligations at church and in our devotions, we got so lost in prayer that He totally invaded our space? That is what He wants to do! What if we became so desperate for more of God that we found a secret place and simply said, "Here I am, God. Now what?"

That is where our family has been lately. We are done with normal. We are ready to see the supernatural. I want to see God's presence poured out on all flesh—not for the sake of seeing miracles, or being seen, or creating a reality show for God. I want to see a God revolution in our nation so that this generation will take Jesus off the crosses they wear around their necks and place Him back on the throne of their lives!

Jesus is not my token or mascot! He is my *Lord.* We have been in services where deaf ears have opened and scars (where cutters have mutilated their arms) have disappeared in the presence of God! Why do we act as though that is not normal? God has more for us than we could ever imagine. He has everything we have ever needed. "No one's ever seen or heard anything like this, never so much as imagined anything quite like it—what God has arranged for those who love him" (1 Cor. 2:9, THE MESSAGE).

He has already given you your victory! If your thirst has brought you to a place of searching for more, then look at what Psalm 107:9 says: "He satisfies the thirsty and fills the hungry with good things." All you need is to hunger and thirst for Him.

STEPS TO BECOMING UNDONE

So, how do you become undone? There are five steps. Let's take a good look at them.

1. Recognize your place of frustration.

By the time Isaiah saw God's throne, he was seriously frustrated. He had nowhere to turn. His mentor, friend, and king had died. Worse than that, the king had died because of pride. (Pride kills. It kills hope, freedom, marriages, relationships between parents and children, and our influence with people.) King Uzziah was Isaiah's cousin. Not only did Isaiah serve the king, but Uzziah was his best friend, his protector, and his identity. For years, Isaiah simply copied whatever the king asked him to say. He was a scribe, the king's personal secretary.

But now, the king was dead and Isaiah was frustrated with his own life and circumstances. He had been living on secondhand information, but those days were now over. Suddenly, he had to find God on his own.

This is how many of us live today. We go to church and say, "Feed me," but we never forage for our own food and drink. God wants to give us *personal* revelation, not hand-me-downs. Being frustrated helps us to get there. It leads us to change; it pushes us to get on our own two feet and move.

It's time to press in and find God on our own. The days of being tossed back and forth by every little wind that blows through the culture are over. Too many of us rely on Facebook, Twitter, and Instagram to be our GPS. We listen and follow whatever is trending for the day. We need to learn how to pursue God on our own as well!

I am directionally challenged, so when I take a trip, I *need* my GPS. But I also bring along a map and directions that I print out ahead of time. Letting the GPS tell me where to go is not enough; I have to be aware of my surroundings and make sure they line up with where I am supposed to be heading.

It's the same in our Christian walk. We can't go through life depending only on the revelation other people get for us. At some point we have to push through and enter God's presence and hear from God for ourselves as well. We have to learn to discern right from wrong and be aware of the signs of the times in which we are living. God's Word provides that direction for us and guides us throughout our journey. It also draws us into a deeper, more intimate relationship with God, our Father.

Isaiah reached a similar tipping point when his cousin, the king, died. Notice what the Bible says about the king: "But after Uzziah became powerful, *his pride* led to his downfall. He was unfaithful to the LORD his God, and entered the temple of the LORD to burn incense on the altar of incense" (2 Chron. 26:16). The king did not die until after he became powerful and prideful. That was the same year in which Isaiah saw the Lord! That is exactly what he said: *"In the year that King Uzziah died,* I saw the Lord high and exalted, seated on a throne; and the train of his robe filled the temple" (Isa. 6:1).

Can you see what happened? According to Isaiah's account, he saw the Lord *in the year that pride died*! Pride is spiritually dehydrating, because when we think we have it all figured out and everything is going our way, we don't recognize our lack or our need for God. Our circumstances provide a false sense of security, and we quit being thirsty. Instead of being desperate for more of God, it becomes about more of us.

What in your life today needs to die in order for you to see God as your King? Is there an area of frustration with your current spiritual or physical condition? Usually that is exactly what pushes you to be thirsty again, as I can testify! At the lowest points in my life, when I have done everything *I can do,* I finally relinquish it all to God. That is when I can hear His voice in the midst of all the noise surrounding me.

That is the power of frustration! The principle also applies at the macro level, as the Bible explains:

> The creation waits in eager expectation for the children of God to be revealed. For the creation was subjected to frustration, not by its own choice, but by the will of the one who subjected it, in hope that the creation itself will be liberated from its bondage to decay and brought into freedom and glory of the children of God.
>
> —ROMANS 8:19–21

Wow! We are sometimes led into frustration so that we might awaken from our slumber, complacency, and neutrality and instead actively pursue freedom and purpose in God!

Frustration is a sign that God has something huge waiting for us! Sometimes He allows us to become frustrated so He can open our eyes to the truth, to our need for Him, and to the need for change. If our lives were always comfortable, we would never budge, and we would miss our moment to see Him, to find freedom, and to lead others to freedom.

Isaiah's frustration, which developed when his security blanket was snatched away by King Uzziah's death, positioned him for change.

2. Come to the place of desperation.

Whenever I get frustrated, I get desperate! Notice what Scripture says: "When I was desperate, I called out, and GOD got me out of a tight spot. GOD's angel sets up a circle of protection around us while we pray" (Ps. 34:6–7, THE MESSAGE).

I love that! Desperation leads to revelation. Have you ever been desperate? If you want to see a desperate person, just look for a mom who has lost sight of her child in a park or a department store. She will drop *everything* to find her missing child. I will never forget when our son Nate was little. He would play tricks and hide in the racks of clothing in department stores. I had to keep a close eye on him at all times. On one occasion, I lost sight of him for what seemed like an eternity. In reality, only a few moments had passed; but it was enough. My heart beat faster and faster as beads of sweat formed on my brow. Unable to find him, I yelled out his name in a panicked tone, "Nate! *Nate!*"

I imagine he could tell by the sound of my voice that

his fun game had gone bad, because he quickly jumped out of a rack of clothing about two aisles over. I snatched him up and kissed him. Then I told him never to leave my sight again.

I suspect that our heavenly Father feels the same way when He sees the enemy trying to draw us into areas that are dangerous for us. That's when He calls out to us in alarm and urges us to come back.

I have heard that alarm sound many times in my spirit. There have been dry and desperate seasons when I was awakened in the middle of the night because I heard God calling my name! Once, Pat and I were sound asleep when I heard someone call my name so loudly, it was like thunder. I thought I was dreaming, but again it thundered: *"Karen!"*

It was loud, but not angry or aggressive. I sat straight up in bed and looked around in the darkness, but I was not afraid. I had heard that voice before, and I knew it was the voice of God.

I had been walking through a season of wondering where God was taking us and what He was specifically calling me to do. I felt that He wanted something more from me; I had been praying in desperation for Him to tell me what it was. I longed for God's presence. The psalmist's words could easily have been mine: "As the deer pants for streams of water, so my soul pants for you, my God" (Ps. 42:1).

That night, God let me know that He was still there and He had a plan. My job was to trust and pursue *Him,* not the plan. Soon after that night, God birthed in me this very book to lead others into the presence of God!

When you finally get desperate enough to lay aside your agenda and decide that all you really want is *Him,* God will speak to you! He is calling out to you today to be desperate for Him. He wants a relationship with you!

We are living in desperate times, so we need to be desperate in our pursuit of God. Nations are rising against nations. Divorce and suicide are at all-time highs. Culture is trying to redefine truth, marriage, and identity. Voices of confusion and humanism are infiltrating a generation at every level, from our schoolhouses to our church buildings. People are searching for answers, but never keeping quiet long enough to hear God speak.

It is time for us to become *undone*! Recently, Reinhard Bonnke met with my husband on a trip to Singapore. He told Pat that unless this generation has an encounter with God, they will never fulfill the prophecy of sons and daughters prophesying (Joel 2:28; Acts 2:17). It's time to become desperate again to see the miraculous. *God loves desperate people*!

Many times, I have identified with these words: "Desperate, I throw myself on you: you are my God!" (Ps. 31:14, THE MESSAGE). My desperation left me absolutely speechless, which in turn opened the door for God to speak.

At times your desperation might leave you feeling imprisoned. That's where I was as a thirteen-year-old girl about to enter the seventh grade. But my "prison break" from fear and insecurity proves that there is no jail that God cannot get you out of. Just call out to Him in your desperation!

> A hard sentence, and your hearts so heavy, and not a soul in sight to help. Then you called out to GOD in your desperate condition; he got you out in the nick of time. He led you out of the dark, dark cell, broke open the jail and led you out. So thank GOD for his marvelous love, for his miracle mercy to the children he loves; he shattered the heavy jailhouse doors, he snapped the prison bars like matchsticks!
> —PSALM 107:12–16, THE MESSAGE

A door of freedom stands before you today. Will you choose to be so desperate as to rise from your circumstances and walk through it? If you will let your faith rise again, it will be tried, proven, and set on display for all to see, just as Scripture says:

> Pure gold put in the fire comes out of it proved pure; genuine faith put through this suffering comes out proved genuine. When Jesus wraps this all up, it's your faith, not your gold, that God will have on display as evidence of his victory.
> —1 Peter 1:7, The Message

Anyone can dance and be moved by music and emotions, but is there evidence to demonstrate a real transformation? Has the proving of your faith produced pure gold in your life? Have you become one who worships to know Him rather than to impress Him? You see, God is looking for people who simply desire Him above everything else.

No matter what your circumstances are, God is calling you to live on purpose and purpose to live!

> Wake up from your sleep, climb out of your coffins; Christ will show you the light! So watch your step. Use your head. Make the most of every chance you get. These are desperate times! Don't live carelessly, unthinkingly. Make sure you understand what the Master wants.
> —Ephesians 5:14–17, The Message

You might ask, "What does He want?" He wants you to want Him. He wants your affection and your heart. He wants you to live free, fully, and abundantly. Stop redecorating the same old tombs in your life and start resurrecting! Stop calling *alive* what God says is dead, and stop calling *dead* what He says is alive.

3. Embrace the moment of confrontation

Once you reach the stage of frustration and desperation, it's time to confront some things in your life. Change
cannot happen until you confront the things that have
held you hostage. Look at Isaiah. He was all alone. No one
was there to see him enter the throne room.

It's crazy sometimes when supernatural things happen
at the altar and our first reaction is to look around and see
what others think. We need to look up in adoration and
gratitude to God who brought us to the place of encounter.

When Isaiah looked around, he found no one to whom
he could brag or boast. It was the perfect recipe for a
supernatural encounter. In response to God's presence,
Isaiah realized how dirty he was. "'Woe is me!" Isaiah
cried. "*I am ruined*! For I am a man of unclean lips, and I
live among a people of unclean lips, and my eyes have seen
the King, the LORD Almighty" (Isa. 6:5).

Notice what Isaiah cried out: "Woe is me!"—not
everyone else, but *me*. He was declaring that he no longer
had a mask or façade to hide behind. He was exposed in
all his unclean ways. That's what happens in God's presence; it reveals *truth*! We have all been fake at some point,
hiding behind our gifts, talents, or abilities. But God is
not fooled. He sees right through our pride and insecurity
and stands ready to heal us. Woe to us if we can't get real
enough to confront the truth!

Here's an excellent piece of advice: don't complain about
what you are unwilling to confront. There is freedom in
confronting your issues and deciding not to be bullied by
the enemy any longer. When you bring into the light what
the enemy has used against you in the dark, it loses its
power to terrorize you!

Confrontation also brings accountability into your
life. Spiritual dehydration ends when you come out from

the shadows and step into the marvelous light. Boldly approach God's throne room for the life-giving refreshment that satisfies rather than pacifies. Examine your heart. What are you refusing to confront in your life? Are you ready to walk away from your past and step into a new season of refreshing? Are you willing to step into freedom? Are you willing to be forgiven?

Maybe these words describe how you feel: "After those years of running loose, I repented. After you trained me to obedience, I was ashamed of my past, my wild, unruly past. Humiliated, I beat on my chest. Will I ever live this down?" (Jer. 31:19, THE MESSAGE).

Some people can't seem to let go of the past in order to see the future. For many, the past has become a crutch, an excuse to keep living the same old way. But continuing to do the same things while expecting different outcomes is a form of insanity! It's time for change! It's time to become undone!

Here is what God wants to do for you: "strengthen your hearts so that you will be blameless and holy in the presence of our God and Father when our Lord Jesus comes with all his holy ones" (1 Thess. 3:13). He will give you the strength to confront the issues that have held you back. You cannot become undone without confronting where you have been.

We have found as we travel across the nation that some people don't want this holy confrontation anymore. It is messy at times and makes us uncomfortable. Our nation is in a compassion crisis right now. We love people's flesh more than we love their souls. We don't want to make them feel bad. Many just want to be told they are great and everything is fine. They want to believe there is nothing to worry about. Too often we accommodate them.

When will we stop being politically correct in order to

avoid confrontation? When will we start telling ourselves and others the truth? There has to be change in our lives. God loves us enough to expose how dirty we are so He can bring us to salvation, healing, and freedom. He loves us that much!

Look what Jesus said about confrontation: "Do you think I came to smooth things over and make everything nice? Not so. I've come to disrupt and confront!" (Luke 12:51, THE MESSAGE).

God is so cool!

4. Reach the moment of revelation

This life is a great journey and adventure with God, so I hope you're ready for the next step! We have come all the way from frustration to desperation to confrontation. Next we arrive at revelation!

There are moments in which you receive true revelation from God. It might be only fifteen minutes of revelation but because it so drastically transforms your heart, it lasts a lifetime. A moment of revelation is not only about information and knowledge, but about experiencing His power and resurrection firsthand. It's the moment you realize that you can be saved. You no longer live in the shade of your grandmother's salvation because you realize that you can have your own relationship with God—a real and loving relationship in which you talk with one another, you can recognize His voice, and you respond.

Are you getting this? God is calling you today to *know that you know that you know* that God is real. He is big. He is the healer. God is your friend, your Father, and the lover of your soul! This is the place Isaiah reached. He was no longer writing down what someone else had seen or heard. His secondhand revelation died with Uzziah. Isaiah wasn't just looking and talking the part—he was *experiencing* God.

Wow! I want to live the God experience, not just talk about it. The experiences I have had with God the Father have convinced me that I can never turn back, turn away from Him, or ever doubt His love for me. I am committed to Him. My life is not my own; I fully submit to the One who gave His life for me. "For I am convinced that neither death nor life, neither angels nor demons, neither the present nor the future, nor any powers, neither height nor depth, nor anything else in all creation, will be able to separate us from the love of God that is in Christ Jesus our Lord" (Rom. 8:38–39).

I'll tell you what I tell people all across this nation: we need a personal glimpse from our Father! We need to enter the place where Daddy looks our way and takes notice. In those moments of revelation we know that we have His full attention—His full affection. When we see the Father's glance, we are changed forever! Nothing says, "Everything is going to be OK" quite like our Father's glance!

I remember when our son Nate was playing high school football. No matter how much noise and commotion was going on around him, Nate could look into the stands and spot his dad cheering him on. It always put in him a fresh fire to go out and play harder.

Pat did his part. He was always there, always focused and making eye contact with Nate at just the right moment. Pat would smile with such pride and affirmation as if to say, "You've got this, Nate. I believe in you, and I stand with you."

Pat does the same thing with Abby. There was a time when Abby was taking ice-skating lessons and needed to test in order to move to the next level. Pat couldn't be there that night because he had a speaking engagement out of town. Abby refused to test without her daddy there because she wanted that support and extra boost of confidence from him. Even though all the other children were getting to move up to the next level, Abby told her teacher that she would wait. She explained that it was important for her daddy to see her succeed.

Pat was there the next week, and she definitely succeeded!

In unsure moments an earthly father's glance can mean so much. It's the look that says, "You can do anything!" How much greater is the glance of our heavenly Father? And His love is calling to you today: "See what great love the Father has lavished on us, that we should be called children of God! And that is what we are!" (1 John 3:1).

Today is our day to catch the glimpse of the Father. Then just like the woman at the well and Isaiah before God's throne, we will be undone and untangled from all the world has used to entrap us. We will finally see who we are really called to be and we'll stop doubting God's power to set us free.

I imagine that was how it felt for the small children whom Jesus called to Himself in Matthew 19:14. It might be how Lazarus felt when he exited the tomb and saw Jesus standing there. It had to have been how Peter felt when the Savior's hand kept him from sinking in the water. You know it had to be how Mary felt as Jesus looked at her from the cross.

As real as His love is, many are prone to seeing the Father as they saw their earthly fathers: angry, condemning, arrogant, unimpressed, or even disappointed. I am here to say: "Take another look!" God does not take His cues from your earthly father. He sees you as He created you to be. He believes in you and is confident that you will get to where He is calling you.

He saw Isaiah that way. So how did the prophet become undone? It wasn't the angels or the thunder. It wasn't even the train of His robe that filled the temple and proved everything must bow to God. What was it then?

It was a face-to-face encounter with his Father!

5. Enter the place of transformation!

God has been waiting for this! You understand frustration and the desperation it causes. You know that they position you for revelation. And now, the fifth step—transformation.

Notice that Isaiah didn't "fit" in the throne room or his earthly surroundings. I love that! God doesn't use the ones everyone else would pick. He chose the strange wild-haired prophet who fit the part, but didn't fit in at all.

For much of my walk with God, I have felt out of place yet in the right place. It's strange, because I didn't fit into my own idea of the "typical" pastor's wife. I had no obvious giftings or talents. I don't sing or play the piano or any instrument, really. My husband and children tell me I sing well, but that's because they want me to cook dinner for them. I'm not sure whether they mean it or are just tone deaf. Or maybe they just love me too much to say otherwise. Whatever the reason, I'm happy that they let me make my joyful noises.

My personality doesn't fit the mold of the "typical" pastor's wife, either. I'm very opinionated and stubborn—not traits that come to most people's minds when they think of a pastor's wife. That's OK though, because what I do possess is a deep longing and desire to know God and lead others to know Him in a real and intimate way. I want to lead those who are bent over in thirst, those whose dry and weary lives have left them wanting. My part is to lead them to the One who will satisfy their thirst forever.

I have been in thousands of services and love watching what God does when His people gather. At times I know the needs of those who are around me. It is a constant struggle for me as a minister to have my own personal encounter during services, because I so desire for others to experience just a taste of what God has for them. Sometimes I feel guilty for watching, but I'm afraid to close my eyes and miss something. I don't want to miss a thing God does!

If you are like me, stop feeling guilty for how you respond to God's presence. It's OK to live in a constant state of excitement and anticipation for what He is about to do—what He can do if people will abandon their pride and allow Him to transform them.

I was standing during a service in Alabama one Sunday as worship and praise filled the sanctuary. It was incredible, yet I noticed that everyone was preoccupied and distracted, talking and fidgeting around in the room. Suddenly, God gave me a vision. I don't say that very often; I am very careful about claiming to have had a vision. In the vision I saw the roof burst open and there on a brilliant white horse sat Jesus, clothed for battle. The horse was snorting and rearing up with its front legs in the air, ready to charge into battle. Jesus held a sword in His right hand and was trying to charge. As long as the people in the sanctuary worshipped with abandon, both horse and rider charged forward. But as the people got distracted and became preoccupied, the horse came to a screeching halt.

This scenario played over and over again. Worship came to an end, but Jesus never made it fully into battle. God spoke to me in that moment. He said that if we would be willing to put aside our plans and agendas and fully enter into worship, abandoning our selfish pride, we would defeat the enemy. So many times we stop too soon and give up before the battle is won. Jesus is doing war in the heavenlies and fighting on our behalf, but we grow weary and give up before the victory is complete.

This has everything to do with transformation. It's time to press in! We need to go further than we have ever gone and push deeper than we thought we could. He is waiting there for us in the secret place.

Jesus doesn't want us to respond to the room around us or the style of music or the lights and videos. All of that is great, but we are to respond as Isaiah responded—to God only! Isaiah was frozen in the midst of God's very presence! His response was to acknowledge God and surrender to Him. He said, "My eyes have seen the King, the LORD Almighty" (Isa. 6:5).

My deepest desire is to see Him, to experience His awesome presence, and to be changed in that moment. Passion and celebration are wonderful, but Isaiah reacted to the presence of God. It is the revelation of who God is that gives us the revelation of who we are supposed to be. We must have His presence. We must have revelation! Then we can be transformed. We will become like Him, to behold Him and encounter Him. As we become brighter in His presence, we will light the path for those who are stumbling in the darkness and trying to find Him.

> Whenever, though, they turn to face God as Moses did, God removes the veil and there they are—face to face! They suddenly recognize that God is a living, personal presence, not a piece of chiseled stone. And when God is personally present, a living Spirit, that old, constricting legislation is recognized as obsolete. We're free of it! All of us! Nothing between us and God, our faces shining with the brightness of his face. And so we are transfigured much like the Messiah, our lives gradually becoming brighter and more beautiful as God enters our lives and we become like him.
>
> —2 CORINTHIANS 3:16–18, THE MESSAGE

A MOMENT AT THE WELL

If you are at a place of frustration today, get in your prayer closet right now. If you are desperate for life-giving water, He is waiting on you! If you are ready to confront the things that have held you back, then He is ready to fight for you. If you are ready for a revelation of the Father's love, His arms are outstretched toward you. He is waiting for you to look into His loving eyes. This is your moment to be transformed. Isaiah had a transforming moment—a salvation moment. You can have that moment right where you are. Just call out to Him and He will answer. God is waiting to wrap His arms around you and begin a new season and relationship with you. Will you accept the invitation to step through the door of freedom? He awaits you!

Chapter 3

FAMINE

*For the word of the LORD holds true, and we can trust
everything he does. He loves whatever is just and
good; the unfailing love of the LORD fills the earth.*

—PSALM 33:4–5, NLT

ARE YOU THIRSTY? We are promised that if we
hunger and thirst for righteousness, we shall be
filled (Matt. 5:6). Yet, I believe that we are now living in
a time of spiritual famine. The biggest cause of famine is
drought. Drought is caused when the heavens no longer
pour out rain. I believe that we must have the latter rain of
God to refresh our land! The psalmist said, "You sent abundant rain, O God, to refresh the weary land" (Ps. 68:9, NLT).

This chapter sounds the alarm. In the Bible famine
causes people to turn back to God. I pray this chapter does
the same for you! It is when we get back to the place of
weeping that God brings forth the rain! Psalm 84:6 says:
"When they walk through the Valley of Weeping, it will
become a place of refreshing springs. The autumn rains
will clothe it with blessings" (NLT). God is getting ready to
clothe His bride with blessings!

I will never forget driving through the desert from
Las Vegas, Nevada to Prescott, Arizona in the summer of
2004. My husband, Pat, was speaking at a youth camp and
we were headed there to meet him for a couple of nights
at the camp. We had just relocated our ministry to Las
Vegas. The move was costly in many ways, but, at the time,

we thought it was the will of God. After arriving in Las Vegas, we quickly realized that we had totally missed it. The church we had relocated to was full of precious people and leaders, but we found that we simply did not fit.

Pat often says, "The calling of God without the timing of God will result in the absence of God!" This was definitely one of those experiences. Nothing seemed to work, and to make matters worse, my daughter Abby, had been sick with various viruses and illnesses from the day we arrived in Nevada. She contracted hand, foot, and mouth disease from the nursery of the church where our ministry was located. I had never heard of such an ailment, but she was very sick from it. And every time we thought she was getting better, she would have a relapse.

More than once during the course of our drive to Arizona, Abby threw up all over herself, the car seat, and the entire car. I drove through the desert with a sick and screaming toddler, our twelve-year-old son, Nate, and my assistant, Jamie. The smell of vomit was overwhelming. For miles on end, there was nowhere to clean Abby or the car, or even to get water. We were in the desert, completely unprepared and at the mercy of our surroundings.

I was in a famine. It had been such a long time since I had truly felt God. I was just going through the motions and hoping for the best. As the chaos calmed down, we all sat in silence; but I wanted to scream. I remember driving the winding roads of the Mojave Desert with tears streaming down my face. I thought to myself, "Where are You, God! Do You even see us? I am literally in a physical and spiritual desert, and I need You. Send Your *rain!*"

DROUGHT HAS A PURPOSE

I will get back to the story, but first let me ask you this question: Have you ever raised your fist in the air and asked God whether He knows your name or even sees you? Have you ever felt as though you were left to die in the desert of your circumstances?

Dry seasons and droughts are not meant to dehydrate or kill us; they are opportunities for us to get up and search out fresh water. Drought causes us to thirst for the right things again. We learn that movement is important; we can't linger in the same pool for too long or the water will become stagnant. Sometimes the well has to dry up so we'll get moving in a new direction. We need fresh water in which to grow and flourish.

New direction means new seasons. Our seasons in life are not meant to last forever. For a period of time, God hid Elijah at the Brook Cherith and sustained him there. "The ravens brought him bread and meat in the morning and bread and meat in the evening, and he drank from the brook" (1 Kings 17:6). But when Elijah needed fresh water, God dried up the brook and gave the prophet further instructions:

> Some time later the brook dried up because there had been no rain in the land. Then the word of the LORD came to him: "Go at once to Zarephath in the region of Sidon and stay there. I have directed a widow there to supply you with food." So he went to Zarephath. When he came to the town gate, a widow was there gathering sticks. He called to her and asked, "Would you bring me a little water in a jar so I may have a drink?" As she was going to get it, he called, "And bring me, please, a piece of bread." "As surely as the LORD your God lives," she replied, "I don't have any bread—only a handful of flour in a jar and a little olive oil in a jug. I am gathering a few sticks to take home and make a meal for myself and my son, that we may eat it—and die."
>
> —1 KINGS 17:7–12

The drying up of the brook forced Elijah out of his comfort zone. He had gotten so comfortable with the blessings God provided that he was willing to go on sitting and receiving instead of actively pursuing what God wanted him to do.

There was a new assignment ahead and it involved the widow. So God sent Elijah to a distant land. But why did God require Elijah to ask for her last bit of food and water in the midst of her greatest lack? I imagine she was at the end of her faith and ready to give up, thinking she was all alone. She probably felt that she had failed her son by not being able to take care of his needs. She probably felt abandoned and cast aside by society.

God not only wanted Elijah's faith activated, He wanted to use Elijah to activate someone else's faith. God wanted to make Himself known to this widow. He wanted to show her that He was her provider, and that with Him, nothing would be impossible. Her husband must have passed away and left her with no resources or income. She had depended on him and others for everything. Now she had no one—no one, but God! He was all she needed.

> Elijah said to her, "Don't be afraid. Go home and do as you have said. But first make a small loaf of bread for me from what you have and bring it to me and then make something for yourself and your son. For this is what the LORD, the God of Israel, says: 'The jar of flour will not be used up and the jug of oil will not run dry until the day the LORD sends rain on the land.'"
> —1 KINGS 17:13–14

God showed Elijah that even in famine, God could use him. Because Elijah was obedient to search for fresh water, he was able to minister life to the widow and encourage and activate her faith. Out of her obedience, she not only received fresh food and water, but she was blessed beyond what she needed. She was then able to provide for someone else's needs, too!

It's time we move beyond our comfort zones and search out the living water, because in our search, we lead others to the life-giving waters they so desperately need. Many, many people are ready to give up and give in to the enemy's lies. They need someone to come along and help them see that life and freedom are found in Christ.

DROUGHT IN OUR MIDST

I believe that our nation and the whole world are in the greatest famine in history. The famine I speak of is not in faraway sub-Saharan Africa or Southern Asia. It is in our midst—and it is much worse than anything we could ever imagine. This famine is in the hearts of men and women who are dehydrated and desperate for the water of the Holy Spirit. It is a famine for truth, and for the Word and presence of God!

Truth is so despised in our culture that it is now seen as hate speech. In this toxic environment, the enemy of truth is silence. People are starved for truth! Pat and I have traveled all across the nation, and everywhere we go, we see people at the altars, bent over with the deep longing for refreshing. They are thirsting for truth—the streams of living water.

The truth changes us. Jesus declared in John 8:32: "You shall know the truth, and the truth shall set you free" (MEV). The woman at the well was desperate for living water. Her encounter with Jesus awakened her to the truth of God's freedom and purpose.

This experience awaits the millions who are desperate for living water today. I am reminded of an old worship song called, "Let It Rain."[1] It describes this desperate thirst and asks the Lord to send His rain and touch His people.

We must awaken this thirsty generation to their season of refreshing! We ought to have a burden for them. There is a prophet in the Bible we rarely hear about. His name is *Amos,* which means "burden-bearer."[2] Amos carried a very heavy burden. He lived in a time when indulgence and perversion had overtaken the people of God.[3] They worshipped God, but had very little relationship with Him, much like many people today.

What I love about Amos is that he came out of nowhere. He didn't come from a long lineage of prophets. He was a simple shepherd and farmer who had a word from God. Amos was a "minor prophet" with a big burden:

> Amos made clear in his writings that he did not come from a family of prophets, nor did he even consider himself one. Rather, he was "a grower of sycamore figs" as well as a shepherd (Amos 7:14–15). Amos's connection to the simple life of the people made its way into the center of his prophecies, as he showed a heart for the oppressed and the voiceless in the world.[4]

Amos longed to awaken a wondering people out of their slumber and complacency. He wrote about injustice and made sure people knew that God was their Judge.

In today's culture we work so hard to tell people about God's love that we forget to remind them that He is also our Judge. Amos did not make that mistake. He knew that destruction was coming and used word pictures to get his message across. He was like the guy who stands on the corner holding a sign that says, "The end is near!" No one wants to make eye contact with a guy like that, but they desperately need to hear from him.

Amos's message got on people's nerves. To the comfortable it was appalling, and to the religious it was disconcerting. Amos was well aware of this and understood the effect he had on them:

> People hate this kind of talk. Raw truth is never comfortable or popular. But here it is, bluntly spoken: Because you run roughshod over the poor and take the bread right out of their mouths, you're never going to move into the luxury homes you have built. You're never going to drink wine from the expensive vineyards you've planted. I know precisely the extent of your violations, the enormity of your sins. Appalling! You bully right-living people, taking bribes right and left and kicking the poor when they're down.
>
> —AMOS 5:11–12, THE MESSAGE

I imagine people scoffed at Amos's message. Yet, I believe that what he wrote roughly 750 years before the birth of Christ applies to our world right now. Like Amos, I am willing to be labeled as "that crazy person on the corner" in order to declare his message to the current generation. Amos saw famine coming and warned others: "The time is coming, says the LORD God, when I will send a famine on the land, not a famine of bread, nor a thirst for water, but of hearing the words of the LORD" (Amos 8:11, MEV).

Why would Amos use the word *famine*? Famine always indicates a water shortage that is followed by a food shortage. The food shortage happens *because* of drought. This is also true in spiritual terms. Jesus said, "Truly, truly I say to you, unless a man is born of water and the Spirit, he cannot enter the kingdom of God" (John 3:5, MEV). Both are necessary—water and Spirit! God is our spring of refreshing, our very life source! Without Him we wander in a desert of destruction and pain.

Jesus told the woman at the well that "whoever drinks of the water that I shall give him will never thirst. Indeed, the water that I shall give him will become in him a well of water springing up into eternal life" (John 4:14, MEV). He also said that her people (the Samaritans) did not know whom they were worshipping (John 4:22). They had no idea what to worship. So when the woman met Jesus she didn't even know what was missing in her life. She was lost and searching for answers because her people, her husbands, and even her false religion had rejected her. She didn't know *what* she believed.

Then she was exposed to Jesus, who knew everything about her. He not only knew her past, but He loved her enough to awaken her future. She was suddenly aware of the living water that He offered, and of her own thirst.

It's time that we allow God to awaken our thirst again! As we pursue the living water, we must lead others to it. So many people are dry, dehydrated, and thirsty for God's presence in their lives. They are looking for leaders who won't just point them in the direction of the living water, but actually join them in the journey to God's well. Then they will be filled there, never to thirst again. They will find their purpose and value in God and be satisfied in Him.

Our journeys are not all about us. In our pursuit of God, we should live so purely and passionately for Him that it produces a thirst for more of God in all whom we encounter. The culture is calling us to worship everything except the one true God. In their search for truth, many have settled for lies that are disguised as the real thing. They think that if it looks good, sounds good, and feels good then it must be true.

It's not. Please be careful not to fall prey to the enemy's

plans. Proverbs 16:25 warns: "There is a way that appears to be right, but in the end it leads to death." We are in constant pursuit of things that can never fulfill us. Without God, fleshly desires, promotion, acceptance, and selfish ambition only leave us empty. He is what we really need. He is the living water that preserves us. Our fulfillment must be in Him and Him alone. We must allow our parched spirits to engage a living God once again.

The Bible declares: "'Come!' say the Spirit and the Bride. Whoever hears, echo, 'Come!' Is anyone thirsty? Come! All who will, come and drink, drink freely of the Water of Life!" (Rev. 22:17, THE MESSAGE).

THE TRUTH ABOUT FAMINE

There is famine in this generation. From the school-house to the church house to the neighbor's house, we see famine. Some say, "Not in America! Not in the most prosperous nation! We have more than enough." I wish they were right, but they are not.

Famine is not always about food. The word *famine* means "any extreme and general scarcity."[5] We have famine in the midst of material abundance. It is a famine for the Word of the Lord. This generation is pursuing everything but God to find refreshing and satisfaction. Yet, our thirst and our cravings seem never to be quenched.

The greatest factor in creating a famine is the lack of fresh water. Our waters have been muddied by untruths. We listen to celebrities and other public figures who say there are many paths to God. No! There is but one way, and that is Jesus Christ. Jesus said: "I am the way and the truth and the life. No one comes to the Father except through me" (John 14:6). He is the only way. We must listen to truth and allow God to restore fresh water—the living water that heals the desert in our midst.

Here is what we must understand: famine is the result of a process that occurs over time and leads to destruction. For example, we have seen the devastation in the nation of Somalia. We see it in pictures of starving children and great injustice. I remember seeing a photo of a child lying on the ground with a giant buzzard close by, waiting for the child's demise. My heart was broken at the devastation and suffering.

How did Somalia end up like this? Oxfam International explains the process that occurred over time:

Famines result from a combination "triple failure":

Production failure: In Somalia, a two-year drought—which is phenomenal in now being the driest year in the last 60—has caused record food inflation, particularly in the expectation of the next harvest being 50% of normal. Somalia already had levels of malnutrition and premature mortality so high as to be in a "normalized" state of permanent emergency. This is also true in pockets across the entire region.

Access failure: The drought has killed off the pastoralists' prime livestock assets (up to 90% animal mortality in some areas), slashing further their purchasing power. In addition Somalia [sic] severe internal conflict has made development almost impossible to achieve and data difficult to access both accurately and credibly.

Response failure: Underlying it all has been the inability of Somalia's government and donors to tackle the country's chronic poverty, which has marginalized vulnerable people and fundamentally weakened their ability to cope. There's been a lack of investment in social services and basic infrastructure

and lack of good governance. Meanwhile donors
have reacted too late and too cautiously. The overall
international donor response to this humanitarian
crisis has been slow and inadequate. According to
UN figures, $1 billion is required to meet imme-
diate needs. So far donors have committed less than
$200m, leaving an $800 million black hole.[6]

Did you catch the three points? They are specific to
Somalia, but we can apply them to other famines. Today's
fundamental famine is our lack of the Word of the Lord!
Without it, we are in trouble. This generation is desperate
for a refreshing. The problem is that, instead of living
water, they are drinking the world's poison.

This is exactly what the prophet Amos described!

On Judgment Day, lovely young girls will faint of
Word-thirst, robust young men will faint of God-
thirst, along with those who take oaths at the
Samaria Sin-and-Sex Center, saying, "As the lord
god of Dan is my witness!" and "The lady goddess of
Beer-sheba bless you!" Their lives will fall to pieces.
They'll never put it together again.
—AMOS 8:13–14, THE MESSAGE

Today's culture perverts even the idea of thirst and
relates it to the craving for sexual sin rather than the
longing for God's presence.[7] Satan always tries to pervert
what God is doing. God intends for thirst to bring us to
His throne room. Satan wants to keep us thirsty for the
world. Thirsting for God brings freedom; thirsting for the
world leads to bondage.

SPIRITUAL FAMINE: THREE CAUSES

Let's explore the famine in our midst in terms of the three
causes of famine attributed to the Somali crisis:

1. We have a production failure.

We are producing a generation so scarred by the pains of childhood that life becomes centered on survival rather than on thriving. They will try anything to get relief from their pain. We are not producing in them a hunger and thirst for the right things. They are looking for pleasure before purpose and freedom *from* man's law rather than freedom *in* God's law.

Some statistics from the 2013 national Youth Risk Behavior Survey should wake us up. Here is just a segment of the survey's results in regard to high school students in the United States:

Sexual risk behaviors

- Forty-seven percent had sexual intercourse.

- Six percent had sexual intercourse for the first time before age thirteen.

- Fifteen percent had sexual intercourse with four or more people during their life.

- Thirty-four percent had sexual intercourse with at least one person during the three months before the survey.

- Forty-one percent did not use a condom during last sexual intercourse.

Alcohol and other drug use

- Twenty-two percent of those who were sexually active drank alcohol or used drugs before last sexual intercourse.[8]

These statistics are astounding. Because we have allowed Hollywood, secular culture, and human pride to seed this generation, Hollywood, the music industry and other media entities, and celebrities have become the standards by which we allow our children to live. Therefore, their lives are producing a harvest of perversion. We must lead this generation toward supernatural encounters with God! But how will they encounter Him unless they see us encounter Him and live out the freedom we profess?

2. We have an access failure.

This is tied to the removal of God from everyday life. Statistics tell the story: "Less than 20% of Americans regularly attend church."[9] God will invade hearts when we are engaged in worship. We must allow the Holy Spirit to flow in our services again; it is not about showing up to fulfill an obligation or ritual! People are desperate for truth. A self-driven message laced with humanism and a passing mention of Jesus will not cut it.

I have seen it. We receive testimonies from all over the world. This generation is desperate to see God move in a powerful and real way. We have seen miracles during God-encountering services. Scars have disappeared from the arms of those who engage in self-harming behaviors. God has shown us that when He does a healing work on the inside, it manifests on the outside. That is why the scars disappear.

We must get away from our prepackaged messages that have little of the Spirit. We have to stop worrying about being politically correct and start speaking the truth in love so that a generation knows where true freedom comes from. They are thirsty for truth and the Word of God. God's messengers must declare truth to them! Jesus promised that the Holy Spirit would guide us into all truth:

> But when he, the Spirit of truth, comes, he will guide
> you into all the truth. He will not speak on his own;

> he will speak only what he hears, and he will tell
> you what is yet to come. He will glorify me because
> it is from me that he will receive what he will make
> known to you. All that belongs to the Father is mine.
> That is why I said the Spirit will receive from me
> what he will make known to you.
>
> —JOHN 16:13–15

Without the Word of the Lord we are doomed to buy into man's concepts and false pretenses. Psalm 33:4 says: "For the word of the LORD is right and true; he is faithful in all he does." God is our compass when we are lost. He is the map for our journey. God is my GPS system, my "God-Positioning System." I already mentioned that I am directionally challenged. The truth is I could probably get lost in a convenience store. I knew my struggle was real when I had to set off my panic alarm to find my car in the Walmart lot. Worse, I often have to ask my twelve-year-old if she remembers where we parked. (She usually does!) I always say that I must have missed the inner GPS part of the assembly line while being formed in my mother's womb. That's why I never leave home without Mapquest directions *and* my GPS.

More importantly I need direction from God's Word to know where to go and how to avoid roadblocks in my faith. His Word is the road map to my life. So why would I ever leave home without preparing a route for that day's success and freedom? I want to be on the path that leads to joy, purpose, and peace in my life.

The enemy always tries to detour our faith. If we remove God from our lives we doom ourselves to wandering in deserts of lost purpose. The prophet Jeremiah described a time when the people found the Word of the Lord offensive. He wrote: "To whom can I speak and give warning? Who will listen to me? Their ears are closed so they cannot

hear. The word of the LORD is offensive to them; they find
no pleasure in it" (Jer. 6:10).

We need to find pleasure in God's Word—to desire His
presence and long for Him. That is my constant goal! God's
presence keeps me sane in a crazy world. Every morning,
my dry and weary soul says: "My heart has heard you say,
'Come and talk with me.' And my heart responds, 'LORD, I
am coming'" (Ps. 27:8, NLT). This is the only way I can stay
refreshed and prevent famine in my life.

We have access failures when our approach to God's
Word is tainted. Our culture is redefining His Word so
that it "lines up" with people's perversions. We must make
a stand against the culture of this world. Culture always
has and always will do the bidding of the god of this age.
God has called us to take a stand!

> The world is unprincipled. It's dog-cat-dog out
> there! The world doesn't fight fair. But we don't live
> or fight our battles that way—never have and never
> will. The tools of our trade aren't for marketing or
> manipulation, but they are for demolishing that
> entire massively corrupt culture. We use our pow-
> erful God-tools for smashing warped philosophies,
> tearing down barriers erected against the truth of
> God, fitting every loose thought and emotion and
> impulse into the structure of life shaped by Christ.
> Our tools are ready at hand for clearing the ground
> of every obstruction and building lives of obedience
> into maturity.
> —2 CORINTHIANS 10:3–6, THE MESSAGE

We have to fight the world's ways every day. Many
have grown weary and have given up. Some well-known
Christian leaders are now reducing God's Word to fleshly,
humanistic messages of false hope that appease our spiritual narcissism. These messages tickle the ears of the

congregation in order to fill seats and grow churches. They have reduced grace to freedom of the flesh without accountability.

This is not truth. We need to understand that Jesus never said we wouldn't go through tough times. In fact, He said the opposite:

> I have told you these things, so that in Me you may have [perfect] peace *and* confidence. In the world you have tribulation and trials and distress and frustration; but be of good cheer [take courage; be confident, certain, undaunted]! For I have overcome the world. [I have deprived it of power to harm you and have conquered it for you.]
> —JOHN 16:33, AMP

Did you get that? Yes! We will have hard times, It is a given. Hard times are part of this life; but hard times cannot harm you! Jesus has got you covered! He's got your back! The Word of the Lord transforms minds, bodies, and souls! Even when we are gone, His Word will remain! "'The word of the Lord remains forever.' And that word is the Good News that was preached to you" (1 Pet. 1:24–25, NLT).

Not everyone still preaches the Word of the Lord. When you remove God's Word, you also remove conviction and truth. God's Word does not bring condemnation; however, it does bring conviction, which in turn brings change.

Where is the change? Recently, a minister in Nashville declared that a "divine wind"[10] from God told him that homosexuality is not a sin. You must understand that what this leader said is absolute blasphemy. God would not speak anything that doesn't align with His Word. God has not asked anyone to rewrite Scripture. This was not the wind of God, but rather a carnal spirit. Jude spoke of a day when men would preach and they would be empty clouds:

> When these people eat with you in your fellowship
> meals commemorating the Lord's love, they are like
> dangerous reefs that can shipwreck you. They are like
> shameless shepherds who care only for themselves.
> They are like clouds blowing over the land without
> giving any rain. They are like trees in autumn that
> are doubly dead, for they bear no fruit and have been
> pulled up by the roots.
>
> —Jude 12, nlt

This describes perverse leaders in no uncertain terms.
In the case of the Nashville pastor already mentioned,
the story gets worse. Now some well-known "Christian"
singers who attend his church have bought into this lie.

The reality is that the truth doesn't always "sell." So
some people choose to flow with winds of compromise
in order to elevate their own agendas. Let me be very
clear: I believe God loves every single person regardless of
whether they are heterosexual or homosexual. God loves
everyone and so should we. But we cannot ask God to love
our sin. He cannot do that. The church must declare the
truth (with love) regardless of whether it offends people's
flesh. We cannot change the message of truth to make
people feel better about their choices. That is the wrong
type of wind; it is called a carnal spirit.

The apostle Paul was very clear on this subject:

> Those who live according to the flesh have their
> minds set on what the flesh desires; but those who
> live in accordance with the Spirit have their minds
> set on what the Spirit desires. The mind governed
> by the flesh is death, but the mind governed by the
> Spirit is life and peace. The mind governed by the
> flesh is hostile to God; it does not submit to God's
> law, nor can it do so. Those who are in the realm of
> the flesh cannot please God.
>
> —Romans 8:5–8

In Romans 7:5 "the Greek word for 'flesh' (*sarx*) refers to the sinful state of human beings, often presented as a power in opposition to the Spirit."[11] The pastor who spoke of a "divine wind" spoke not with the pneuma wind of God, but with a carnal spirit!

We have to discern the wind. Not every wind is the *right wind*. In agriculture the wind can erode the land and cause it to be unproductive. We must arrest *wrong winds* and keep them from eroding this generation and causing famine.

Farmers often plant large trees along their property lines. These trees interfere with the wind and prevent it from eroding the soil.[12] We are to be like those trees. The prophet Isaiah said, "They will be called oaks of righteousness, a planting of the LORD for the display of his splendor" (Isa. 61:3). But we must be planted close to the water source so that we are not blown away by false teachings.

God expects us—and especially leaders—to tell the truth! I am reminded of what the prophet Malachi said concerning ministers who fail to tell the truth:

> It's the job of priests to teach the truth. People are supposed to look to them for guidance. The priest is the messenger of GOD-of-the-Angel-Armies. But you priests have abandoned the way of priests. Your teaching has messed up many lives. You have corrupted the covenant of priest Levi. GOD-of-the-Angel-Armies says so. And so I am showing you up for who you are. Everyone will be disgusted with you and avoid you because you don't live the way I told you to live, and you don't teach my revelation truly and impartially.
>
> —MALACHI 2:7–9, THE MESSAGE

Unless we present both Spirit and truth, there will be a continuing access failure and a diminishing thirst. It is time to allow the Holy Spirit to move among us. It is also time to bring the true Word of God to the culture. Then the dehydrated will realize they are thirsty—not for any wind of doctrine, but for the living water.

3. We have a response failure

We have to awaken from our sleep. This generation needs an alarm clock to go off.

> Up on your feet! Take a deep breath! Maybe there's life in you yet. But I wouldn't know it by looking at your busywork; nothing of *God's* work has been completed. Your condition is desperate. Think of the gift you once had in your hands, the Message you heard with your ears—grasp it again and turn back to God. If you pull the covers back over your head and sleep on, oblivious to God, I'll return when you least expect it, break into your life like a thief in the night.
> —REVELATION 3:2–3, THE MESSAGE

God is looking for those who will bring fresh water to a dry and thirsty land. Who will sound the alarm? My husband recently wrote a book entitled *I Am Remnant* on how to stand for truth in a changing culture. It is time for the remnant to rise once again and lead a generation to the well! It is time that we stand and declare His Word with power and authority. We must tell this generation that eternity is the promise from God. Notice what the apostle John wrote:

> Don't love the world's ways. Don't love the world's goods. Love of the world squeezes out love for the Father. Practically everything that goes on in the

world—wanting your own way, wanting everything for yourself, wanting to appear important—has nothing to do with the Father. It just isolates you from him. The world and all its wanting, wanting, wanting is on the way out—but whoever does what God wants is set for eternity.

—1 JOHN 2:15–17, THE MESSAGE

Together we can stop the famine. We must get back on our knees and pray for rain! For too long we have desired to be known rather than to know Him.

Recently God stirred Pat's heart deeply. Upon finishing prayer, the Lord spoke to him: "Pat, your shoes should not be worn in the heel from chasing man's approval, but scuffed in the front from bended knees that are pursuing Jesus!"

That's it! We must have a holy encounter with God if we are going to become whole again. Our homes need open heavens to pour out God's awesome love, favor, and conviction.

THE RAIN IS COMING

The news around the world is bad! Whether it is about terrorists taking over cities, the economy continuing in free fall, or another judge legislating from the bench, things are getting worse.

Godly families and the church are the trees, the oaks of righteousness that God will use to stop the erosion of the soil in our land. We must take our families by the hand and lead them into God's presence on a daily basis. Our churches must dust off the altars they use as props and let them be places of encounter once again. It's time to have moments in our homes in which we turn off the TVs and the computers, put down our phones, and teach our children how to cry out to God and touch heaven!

The world is in famine, but God has prepared a drink for us right in the midst of it! The following passage says so:

"If you'll hold on to me for dear life," says GOD, "I'll get you out of any trouble. I'll give you the best of care if you'll only get to know and trust me. Call me and I'll answer, be at your side in bad times; I'll rescue you, then throw you a party. I'll give you a long life, give you a long drink of salvation!"
—PSALM 91:14–16, THE MESSAGE

This is exactly what God did for our family when we felt abandoned in the middle of the desert in Las Vegas, Nevada. As I cried out to God, "Do You even see us?" He did see us, and He walked us through that season. God stepped in and revealed that we needed to step back under the blessing. We needed to get back to where we were supposed to be. We were not supposed to be in Las Vegas; we were supposed to be in Birmingham, Alabama.

One thing I have learned on my journey with God is that there is a reason for every season in our lives. But every season must come to an end in order to make room for new life and new growth. During that dry season, I continually heard Him say to me, "Karen, hold on. I am right here. You're not alone! I've got a plan."

God is so full of grace and mercy, and I'm so grateful and thankful that He never leaves us where He finds us. This, for our family, would become one of the greatest seasons of learning to hear His voice. It would also become one of the greatest bonding seasons we would ever experience.

We spent three long months in that desert, but rain was on its way. Late one afternoon after Pat flew in from preaching, there were no words to express the dehydrated state of our souls. Thank God my husband always knows how to bring life and encourage us when we seem lost. That day he walked into the room and declared that we would dance in the middle of where the enemy had tried to take us out. He declared that we would find the rain clouds in the middle of our desert.

Pat took Abby (who was only eighteen months old) into his arms, and I took our son Nate by the hands. We just danced. Then Pat and I held each other and danced. Our family danced and worshipped for what seemed like hours, and we held each other until joy entered our home again.

Within a few short days, we had such clarity and direction on where God was taking us! Our brook had definitely dried up, but we knew God was providing a greater river of life for us. All we had to do was follow where He was leading. I look back at that three-month season as a place to learn God's voice and grow and mature in Him. We couldn't depend on man's provision for what God wanted to provide. We couldn't compromise for what seemed like advancement. We needed to advance God's purpose and in that we would be taken care of. We had to learn to trust God and hear His voice and walk out our faith.

Shortly after this experience we relocated our ministry to Birmingham where we stepped into a higher calling, a new level of ministry, and a fresh season of joy, freedom, and refreshing. But it was back there, in the middle of an actual desert, that we felt the rain of God fall on our dry, weary, and parched lives.

Our desert experience led us to the most refreshing fountain of hope. We also entered into a new season of blessing and favor so that everything we had lost in the move was restored to us. Through that season we kept worship music playing softly in the background twenty-four hours a day, reminding us that He is always there, always calling to us, and all we really need.

We moved on with our life and ministry, but that season taught me what a spiritual famine was really like. I learned that we must crawl through the desert of disappointment, shame, and disillusionment and find His river of living water, as the prophet Isaiah declared:

> Forget about what's happened; don't keep going over old history. Be alert, be present. I'm about to do something brand-new. It's bursting out! Don't you see it? There it is! I'm making a road through the desert, rivers in the badlands. Wild animals will say "Thank you!"—the coyotes and the buzzards—because I provided water in the desert, rivers through the sun-baked earth, Drinking water for the people I chose, the people I made especially for myself, a people custom-made to praise me.
>
> —ISAIAH 43:18–21, THE MESSAGE

The experiences we face are meant to push us closer to the Father, not destroy us. We can cherish every step of our journey because it strengthens us and makes us who we are. It makes us stronger.

I believe with everything within me that God is about to pour out His Spirit in our land in ways we have never seen or imagined. There is a harvest coming! The kingdom of God will experience the latter rain! It is promised in His Word:

> Be glad then, you children of Zion, and rejoice in the Lord, your God; for He gives you the former or early rain in just measure and in righteousness, and He causes to come down for you the rain, the former rain and the latter rain, as before.
>
> —JOEL 2:23, AMP

A MOMENT AT THE WELL

Are you in a famine today? Separate yourself from the fleshly culture of this world. Grab an umbrella or better yet, a bucket! Get ready for the rain of God's presence to fall and wash over your life. Your famine is coming to an end! It's time not only to be refreshed, but to flourish and grow again. It's time for our nation to flourish and grow again!

Chapter 4

REDIG THE ANCIENT WELLS

Isaac reopened the wells that had been dug in the time of his father Abraham, which the Philistines had stopped up after Abraham died, and he gave them the same names his father had given them.

—**GENESIS 26:18**

Tᴀᴇ ᴇɴᴇᴍʏ ᴡᴏᴜʟᴅ love to throw dirt in your well and steal your freedom and life source. He would love to stop up the well that once flowed freely in your life and your family's life. The number one goal of Satan is to snuff out and destroy your legacy and family inheritance.

If he can keep you dry and weary, you will never experience the living water. That is a sobering thought! I love what my husband, Pat, wrote in his book *I Am Remnant*: "The remnant has decided that, at all cost, they will not allow the next generation to speak of the last generation as a group that didn't want to see God's glory."[1] May we be that remnant!

Our desire and focus is to make sure the next generation does not forget who God is. They must not forget that He is the one true God! How we live and present the gospel to them will determine whether our children's children will thirst after the living God. It will determine whether they will experience God's glory or wander in the desert, aimless and hopeless.

If we are going to defeat the enemy's drought then we

need to push past the dirt! I want my family to surpass all that anyone thought we would do. I want us to go farther than I ever imagined we were capable of going. I want to do whatever God has called us to do regardless of what it costs.

Our family believes in spiritual heritage! If you do not come from a family with a long spiritual heritage, then it's time to start one. You can be the first in your family line to seek God and follow Him in truth, power, and authority. It's time to start a new legacy for your family. God is a God of generations—the father of Abraham, Isaac, and Jacob! "But from everlasting to everlasting the LORD's love is with those who fear him, and his righteousness with their children's children..." (Ps. 103:17).

I believe that God is about to start a generational movement in our land. In a time when Christianity is under fire and God's people are being persecuted, it's time to rise up and declare that God is still on the throne, both in our lives and in our nation. I believe there will be an awakening that crosses age barriers. It will move from the nurseries to the nursing homes.

This chapter is about being ready; it is a call to enter into deep alignment with God. The old life has to pass away and a new life has to begin. But first, we must clean out the wells!

THE FIGHT FOR A GENERATION

You are fighting an old foe. Satan is a liar (John 8:44). From the very beginning he has focused on destroying the seed of Adam. Today, the spirit of antichrist is running rampant, not only in the world but also in the church.

The enemy does not want this generation to experience the freedom of the Holy Spirit. In a day of microwave, flesh-driven, man-exalted services, we have removed the God encounter from our gatherings. As a result, our gatherings do not change the people's state of deprivation, but only serve as a reprieve from the realities of their lives.

In many quarters church is somewhere to feel good and fulfill a social commitment. Churches are supposed to be armories where we are equipped and prepared for the battle that is unleashed on us and our families by the enemy. Church is supposed to help us grow and develop our walk with God; it should draw in those who are searching for the answers only He can give.

The enemy is relentless in his quest for us to lose sight of the truth and fail. His objective isn't new. For millennia, he has drawn people away from God, as Scripture attests: "My people have committed a compound sin: they've walked out on me, the fountain of fresh flowing waters, and then dug cisterns—cisterns that leak, cisterns that are no better than sieves [strainers used for sifting]" (Jer. 2:13, THE MESSAGE).

We bring people to the place where living water should be flowing, only to have it leak through their fingers because truth is lacking. It's time our churches got back in the fight and joined the ranks on the front lines of battle.

If we ever really catch hold of who God has called us to be, things will get dangerous for the enemy. We need to quit playing dead and hoping that someone else will fight our battles for us. We talk and talk about revival and revolution, but it's time for action. We need to rise to the challenge. It's not about buildings and technology and programs, as wonderful as those are. It is time for the church to once again preserve the true Word of God and equip the next generation to stand for truth and righteousness. In the current culture truth is no longer deemed relevant. Instead, truth is whatever we decide it should be for the sake of our own convenience. That is a dangerous position to take in an increasingly perilous world.

Children, time is just about up. You heard that
Antichrist is coming. Well, they're all over the place,
antichrists everywhere you look. That's how we
know that we're close to the end. They left us, but
they were never really with us. If they had been, they
would have stuck it out with us, loyal to the end.
In leaving, they showed their true colors, showed
they never did belong. But you belong. The Holy
One anointed you, and you all know it. I haven't
been writing this to tell you something you don't
know, but to confirm the truth you do know, and to
remind you that the truth doesn't breed lies.
                              —1 JOHN 2:18–21, THE MESSAGE

To the degree that we have failed to uphold truth, we
have done a disservice to the generation coming up after
us. Here is what Leonard Ravenhill said about our current state:

The human dilemma that we are in right now is
that we have never been in a lower point. People
say... "Don't worry, we have got out of situations
like this." Oh, no! We haven't. Don't you fool yourself. We've never gotten out of [a] situation like
this. You know why? Because, we have never been
in a situation like this. That's why!...Sex is a sport.
Immorality is an accepted way of life. People say
there are fewer divorces than last year. Well, how
do you expect any more when they don't get married?...So we are a broken nation. Never, never in
our history did we need revival more than today,
the day in which we live.[2]

What we need now is a revival of holiness. A revival of
character. A revival of people who are utterly selfless
and prepared to lay their lives on the altar for God.[3]

Our wells are stopped up, and it's time to unplug them! Someone has to pick up a shovel and dig. This is important to the church, but also to our families. God wants to bless us and our descendants. He wants to initiate a legacy of freedom in our lineages that will carry on for generations to come. God spoke to Abraham about this very thing:

> I will surely bless you and make your descendants as numerous as the stars in the sky and as the sand on the seashore. Your descendants will take possession of the cities of their enemies, and through your offspring all nations on earth will be blessed, because you have obeyed me.
> —GENESIS 22:17–18

God made amazing promises to Abraham, the patriarch of his family. Some of the promises God gives our families are so powerful! But we must realize that the enemy will stop at nothing to steal both the promises and our seed.

Some of you know exactly what I'm talking about. You have had piles of dirt dumped in your wells again and again. You can't seem to shovel it out fast enough. The enemy has worn you out and you are weary in the fight. Don't give up! Keep fighting and keep digging. You will hit water at just the right time. Don't let the enemy steal your seed or the next generation.

ENTERING THE BATTLE

In the summer of 2009 our family vacationed at the beach. Each morning, Pat and I headed to the local track to run or most often, walk and pray. As we walked one morning, we were both unusually quiet. We had become increasingly busy while pastoring the church we started in

Birmingham, and we needed this vacation to regroup and spend time together as a family.

It is easy to become so preoccupied by the tyranny of the urgent that we forget to breathe and enjoy the journey. We took time away at the beach for that very reason. The shore has always been my happy place far away from a hectic schedule. I love doing my devotions on the condo balcony, talking to God and watching in awe as waves crash against the shoreline. God's amazing creation never ceases to amaze me. In that atmosphere I can get lost in its beauty and His presence.

Usually our family vacations focus on catching up with one another, goofing off, and laughing together. This particular morning was different. Pat and I were both visibly distracted as we walked the track together. Finally he looked at me and said, "I had a disturbing dream last night."

I said, "Me, too, but you go first."

He proceeded to say that he dreamed our son Nate was killed in an accident. He also shared that the dream was weighing heavily on him. Immediately tears welled up in my eyes. I looked at Pat and said that I'd had a similar dream. I'd dreamed that Nate was in a car accident and was presumed dead. In my dream, we couldn't find Nate. He was lost.

I don't believe every dream is from God. Some dreams are caused by too much pizza or an overactive imagination triggered by things we watch or discuss before bed. However, I *do believe* in prophetic dreams. Usually I can't remember the details of my dreams. When I do, I know that God is trying to tell me something. These are the dreams I cannot seem to get out of my mind and heart all day. So I keep a dream journal, and after I write them down, I wait for God to reveal the meaning. He always does. It might be a few days or a few years, but He always reveals the meaning right when I need it.

When Nate was a baby, I had a similar dream about him. In that one, I realized the enemy would try to kill Nate in order to prevent his God-ordained destiny from unfolding. Satan did in fact try to accomplish his goal through infant asthma and a car accident when Nate was two. God has clearly had His hand upon both our children!

The enemy hates God's destiny for your kids. He will do anything to destroy it!

Pat and I refuse to believe that God would allow our children's destiny to be altered. So we keep them covered in prayer. Because the nature of the dreams we had during our vacation was concerning to us, we immediately went into prayer and intercession for Nate.

I don't believe that just because we are in ministry our kids will automatically follow what we do as parents. They *will* be tempted. I believe that we have to war in the spirit for them and show them by example the path to freedom, joy, and purpose. Our children need to have their own encounters with God; but we must make sure they are in the right atmosphere for that to happen. If they swerve off the right path, we need to be there so we can help them get back on track.

About a week after Pat and I had our disturbing dreams, Nate came and confessed that, for about three months, he had not been living as he should. He told us he had been in a war during a period of football recruiting and had gotten caught up in things he knew were not right. It was eating away at him and he could not continue living a lie. He was miserable and had lost his peace and joy. He needed to be free again. He needed us to pray with him and help him get back to where he wanted and needed to be spiritually.

We were thankful that Nate opened up, but we were completely shocked and caught off guard. Our dreams from the prior week made sense now. They were not about physical death, but a spiritual one. Nate was being attacked by the enemy; the fight for his spirit was on. He was being pulled in the wrong direction and was getting lost. We needed to spring into action to get him back.

That began a journey of war between us and the enemy to take back our son and declare that he was an overcomer and a champion. Nate is a powerful young man. He was determined that his destiny would not be decided by mistakes he had made during a dry season in his life. In that season he had dropped his guard and let the pull of the crowd draw him in, but I am so grateful that he heard the voice of God calling him back.

Nate knew God's voice; he had heard it before and had had encounters with God, even at two years old, sitting in his car seat. I can remember him back then talking to Jesus, giving Him a hug, and telling me that Jesus had hugged him back. God knew Nate as a baby, and He still had great and powerful plans for him. There were many nights that we stayed up praying, talking, and walking with Nate to freedom—not only from sin but from the feelings of failure and from the guilt and condemnation the enemy was using to keep Nate down when he was meant to stand tall. Nate had completely turned away from the things that had enticed him; God had already convicted Nate, brought him to repentance, and forgiven him. However, Nate found it hard to forgive himself.

It was time to redig the ancient wells that said we and our children were more than overcomers, the head and not the tail. God had promised Pat and me that our kids would serve the Lord. They would be victorious and would be among those who change the world.

We were not about to let those promises die! However, as we continued to minister and travel and do what God had called us to do, the enemy continued kicking dirt into our well. How could this happen? How could we not have seen the signs? How could we have allowed our son to be drawn into the world and not even know it? Had we become so consumed and busy with the work of the Lord that we had let something slip by us?

In our busyness, we sometimes have to stop what we are doing and go to war! That means getting down on our knees, clearing the calendar, scratching off all appointments, and saying, "Wait a minute! *Enough!*" God is more powerful than any failures we might have.

When our call to war came, I was angry at the devil. The one thing I was sure of was that Satan would not win. If it was war he wanted, then Pat and I were ready to suit up in full armor and fight! You don't mess with our babies and get away with it. We have read the ending of the Book and it says, "We *win!*"

Coming Full Circle in Blessing

Every day after our children went off to school, Pat and I would head to the high school track. There we began to dig and dig and dig, quoting scriptures and speaking life over our family. When Pat was out of town speaking at a conference, I would run alone, wearing my headphones, worshipping, praying, crying, and even beating my fists on the pavement at times.

We would not give up. We realized that somewhere along the way we must have lost sight of what really mattered. Now it was time to get back to the well and drink. That track became our well.

Those mornings of pouring my heart out and warring for my child reminded me of the Samaritan woman at the well.

This was my long daily walk in search of answers. On that track I met the Man, my Savior. He knew Pat and me. He knew what we were facing. He also knew our son and the destiny and calling on his life. He knew where Nate had been, but He had the power to set him back on the right track.

Just as Jesus met the Samaritan woman at the well, He met me at that track each day and the two of us ran together. At first these mornings were all about crying out and pouring out my petitions to God. They became times of rejoicing and worshipping and raising my hands in the air in love, adoration, and gratitude for how Jesus had so transformed Nate's life, setting him on the right path and filling him with joy, passion, and purpose again.

Our son was set free! In his book *Why Is God So Mad at Me?* Pat shares the story of how Nate got free and how Pat led him on a journey of leaving the past behind and walking into a new season of freedom. That quest has led Nate, his wife, Adrienne, and our grandson, Jack, into leading a generation of youth to freedom and true relationship with a loving Father God! Nate shares his testimony with thousands of young people and athletes in schools. He bears witness as the light comes on and they realize they can be free and in loving relationship with God. They learn that they can overcome too.

We had the privilege of witnessing the ultimate slap in the devil's face in May, 2014. Pat had gone away for a few days to finish up work on a book. When he was done, I joined him for a little getaway during which we watched online as our son spoke to a large youth convention in Canada.

It just so happened that this particular convention was the very first youth convention Pat had spoken at after we accepted the call to evangelism many years earlier! Nate was a small child at that time. Now, as we watched him preach with such power, authority, and purity, we were amazed and *very* blessed. I remembered how the enemy had attacked him with illness and injury, and how he tried to snuff him out—*but God!* Now Nate was a thorn in the devil's side as young people ran to the altar, crying out to God.

Pat looked over at me and said, "Wow. That was the most powerful sermon I have ever heard."

God brought Nate full circle as he preached at the very place where his dad and I had started out. We dug the well; now Nate was drinking from it and keeping it flowing. What generational blessings and favor!

DEFENDING THE WELLS

Has dirt been dumped into your wells? Is the junk piling up so high that you can barely see the light of day? Many of you reading this book think your inheritance has been stolen. But are you willing to pick up a shovel and dig for it?

An account from the Book of Genesis talks about redigging wells. Let's examine the story in sections:

> Now there was a famine in the land—besides the previous famine of Abraham's time—and Isaac went to Abimelek king of the Philistines in Gerar. The LORD appeared to Isaac and said, "Do not go down to Egypt; live in the land where I tell you to live. Stay in this land for a while, and I will be with you and will bless you. For to you and your descendants I will give all these lands and will confirm the oath I swore to your father Abraham. I will make your descendants as numerous as the stars in the sky and will give them all these lands, and through your offspring all nations on earth will be blessed, because Abraham obeyed me and did everything I required of him." So Isaac stayed in Gerar.
>
> —GENESIS 26:1–6

God gave Isaac clear instructions that were designed to benefit him. It was up to Isaac to obey. Likewise, we must return to what God has told us to do, obeying His law so that we will be blessed. In times of crisis, we need to be able to say, "We have followed the commands of God and we are claiming His blessings. This is God's promise to us."

Read what happened when Isaac followed God's instructions:

> Isaac planted crops in that land and the same year reaped a hundredfold, because the LORD blessed him. The man became rich, and his wealth continued to grow until he became very wealthy. He had so many flocks, and herds and servants that the Philistines envied him. So all the wells that his father's servants had dug in the time of his father Abraham, the Philistines stopped up, filling them with earth. Then Abimelek said to Isaac, "Move away from us; you have become too powerful for us."
> —GENESIS 26:12–16

Isaac's obedience led to great abundance! The Philistines were not happy about it, so they stopped up the wells Isaac's father, Abraham, had dug. Then their king asked Isaac to leave the land.

There may come a time when the anointing on your life will not be received by the people you hang out with. You might have to move away. That was true in Nate's case. While he had gotten free from the entanglements his enemy used against him, he needed to put distance between himself and the familiar spirits that had enticed him. He stayed strong and went off to Southwestern University. There he was able to focus on the plans God had for him as he grew and matured into the man of power and purpose he was called to be.

That is very similar to what happened to Isaac. He had become powerful and was reaping the blessings of living a life for God. The Philistines were jealous of him and Abimelek feared that Isaac was becoming too powerful.

> So Isaac moved away from there and encamped in the Valley of Gerar, where he settled. Isaac reopened the wells that had been dug in the time of his father Abraham, which the Philistines had stopped up after Abraham died, and he gave them the same names his father had given them. Isaac's servants dug in the valley and discovered a well of fresh water there. But the herders of Gerar quarreled with those of Isaac and said, "The water is ours!" So he named the well Esek, because they disputed with him. Then they dug another well, but they quarreled over that one also; so he named it Sitnah. He moved on from there and dug another well, and no one quarreled over it. He named it Rehoboth, saying, "Now the LORD has given us room and we will flourish in the land." From there he went up to Beersheba. That night the LORD appeared to him and said, "I am the God of your father Abraham. Do not be afraid for I am with you; I will bless you and will increase the number of your descendants for the sake of my servant Abraham." Isaac built an altar there and called on the name of the LORD. There he pitched his tent, and there his servants dug a well. Meanwhile, Abimelek had come to him from Gerar, with Ahuzzath his personal adviser and Phicol the commander of his forces. Isaac asked them, "Why have you come to me, since you were so hostile to me and sent me away?" They answered, "We saw clearly that the LORD was with you; so we said, 'There ought to be a sworn agreement between us'—between us and you. Let us make a treaty with you that you will do us no harm, just as we did not harm you but always

treated you well and sent you away peacefully. And
now you are blessed by the LORD." Isaac then made
a feast for them, and they ate and drank. Early the
next morning the men swore an oath to each other.
Then Isaac sent them on their way, and they went
away peacefully. That day Isaac's servants came and
told him about the well they had dug. They said,
"We've found water!" He called it Shibah, and to this
day the name of the town has been Beersheba."

—GENESIS 26: 17–33

Isaac moved away, and his enemies attacked his wells
again. Why do I share this account with you? To show you
the importance of keeping the wells of revival open, and
to show you that you have to keep digging to find fresh
water, blessings, and favor.

We don't know much about Isaac, but we know he was
a well redigger! He was thirsty and was determined to dig
the wells that his father had established. We also know
that Isaac walked in awesome favor. Wherever he went he
saw miracles and was blessed. Why? Isaac's dad, Abraham,
had paid the price for Isaac. He followed God and obeyed
Him; because of it, his family was blessed.

Isaac obviously learned from his father and was determined to redig the wells of favor and relationship with
God that his father had dug. The Philistines covered up
the wells, but only after Abraham had died. The question is: why, when water was so scarce would anyone fill
up good wells with dirt? It was obvious that without that
water, people would die!

The reason is simple: the Philistines were the enemies
of God's people. They wanted to wipe His people out.
Plugging up the wells that Abraham had dug was a way of
getting the job done.

This is exactly what Satan is doing to Christians and

churches across our nation today. Make no mistake: he wants to wipe you out! So he tries to fill the wells of your spirit with dirt and worldly junk to cut off your life and water source, which is from God.

The Philistines filled Abraham's wells with earth, which represents the flesh. Wells represent the life-giving Word of God. The Philistine spirit is operating in the church today and has diluted the anointed, life-giving Word of God with fleshly, carnal teachings which impart knowledge without revelation. The people are perishing because they have been robbed of their vision of life. It is time to stop the enemy from killing the blessing that should be passed to the next generation.

The next generation must experience the wells! You and I must pass the wells on to them. We cannot allow our family wells to be covered with dirt. I know I want my kids to hear my husband and me praying and interceding for them. I want them to experience the miracles and the blessings. I want them not only to hear, but also to see what God is doing across the land. I want Nate and Abby and our grandson, Jackson, to meet people of all ages who say, "Your mom and dad made a difference. They lived what they preached, and it was real!"

I want our children and grandchildren to know that we dug wells for our family. They need to know that if they will continually return to these wells (and to the King of kings from whom they spring) they will never ever thirst again.

The wells of Abraham had been stopped up by the enemies of God. The Philistine king pressed Isaac to leave his land. The Philistines were enemies of God. They would continue to mount pressure against Isaac. It was Isaac's job to redig the wells and take back the land. He had to set right what the enemy had destroyed.

It's time that we as Christians arise and take back

the land that the enemy has stolen from us. Culture,
humanism, and fleshly desires have taken over our nation
and filled our wells with dirt. It's time to dig those wells
again! We cannot back down. We must keep digging and
resist the all-out war that is designed to keep our nation
and our families from God's blessing and destiny!

We will succeed if we drink from righteous wells and
not the world's toxic ones. "The Fear-of-GOD is a spring of
living water so you won't go off drinking from poisoned
wells" (Prov. 14:27, THE MESSAGE).

Are you getting this? God is all about generational blessings and legacy. What I do today determines the future
of my children and their children. I can't live according
to my own selfish desires but rather by the leading of the
Holy Spirit. I want to dig a well so deep that, for generations to come, my family will know how to get the living
water that never runs dry.

THREE WELLS

The account of Isaac's struggle with the Philistines reveals
three wells that we must dig.

Well #1: Esek (Meaning "Dispute[4] or Argument")

When Isaac's servants uncovered a certain well, "the
herders of Gerar quarreled with those of Isaac and said,
'The water is ours!' So he named the well *Esek*, because
they disputed with him" (Gen. 26:20).

Listen! When you redig wells of favor and blessing,
expect an argument and a fight! Of course the enemy
opposes this. It is time to argue and fight back! That is
what Pat and I did when our son was being attacked. We
disputed the enemy's plot to destroy our family. This is
what the Bible means when it says: "We demolish arguments and every pretension that sets itself up against the

knowledge of God, and we take captive every thought to make it obedient to Christ" (2 Cor. 10:5).

Satan wants your inheritance! He will do everything he can to steal and destroy it. You have to be strong and courageous, ready to defend your faith and stand against those who would deceive and argue against what is true and just. There is no room for shrinking back; you must move forward and stand strong.

> This resurrection life you received from God is not a timid, grave-tending life. It's adventurously expectant, greeting God with a childlike "What's next, Papa?" God's Spirit touches our spirits and confirms who we really are. We know who he is, and we know who we are: Father and children. And we know we are going to get what's coming to us— an unbelievable inheritance! We go through exactly what Christ goes through. If we go through the hard times with him, then we're certainly going to go through the good times with him!
> —ROMANS 8:15–17, THE MESSAGE

Well #2: Sitnah (Meaning "Strife[5] or Opposition")

"Then [Isaac's servants] dug another well, but [the herdsman of Gerar] quarreled over that one also; so [Isaac] named it *Sitnah*" (Gen. 26:21). When you redig the wells that are rightfully yours, you will face opposition and strife! When you finally decide that you are going to live free, serve God, and bring your family back into alignment with His Word, opposition will come from every direction.

The enemy does not like to lose a fight. He certainly does not like to lose control over those he has fought to keep in bondage. While you were in bondage to sin, pain, and destruction, you were not a threat to Satan. Therefore, he didn't bother you. Now, you are a threat and you can expect him to notice.

But don't lose hope. Fix your eyes on Jesus, the author and perfecter of your faith! (See Hebrews 12:2.) The enemy has a shovelful of dirt he wants to throw in your well, so be alert. "Guard the good deposit that was entrusted to you—guard it with the help of the Holy Spirit who lives in us" (2 Tim. 1:14).

Satan has strategically placed temptations in the culture that are designed to destroy your children by first enticing them away from the wells that you have dug for the family. The devil was a murderer from the beginning (John 8:44). He is a dream-slayer who sneaks in through every day means, including technology, media, and music. We have to be alert, because through these common access points, Satan is shoveling dirt into our wells and planting seeds of discouragement, worthlessness, confusion, lust, and degradation.

Just by watching television commercials and other advertisements, our children are exposed to a regular diet of pornography. We have accepted them as the norm. It's time to confront the opposition and say, "No more! We are taking back our families!"

Well #3: Rehoboth (Meaning "Enlargement and Flourishing"⁶ or Room to Live Freely and Expand)

> He moved on from there and dug another well, and no one quarreled over it. He named it Rehoboth, saying, "Now the LORD has given us room and we will flourish in the land." From there he went up to Beersheba.
> —GENESIS 26:22–23

You cannot give up, lie down, or surrender to the enemy. You must keep digging, pressing in, and pursuing God's presence. You have to continually return to the well until you break through and break out of the chains in which the enemy has kept your family for generations.

When you redig your wells, the enemy will try to move in on your territory. You will face arguments and opposition. But eventually—because you refused to quit—your territory will be enlarged. You will flourish because you have room to live freely, expand, and take authority over the enemy in your life. You will become like a well-watered garden, the blessing that Isaiah described:

> If you get rid of unfair practices, quit blaming victims, quit gossiping about other people's sins, if you are generous with the hungry and start giving yourselves to the down-and-out, your lives will begin to glow in the darkness, your shadowed lives will be bathed in sunlight. I will always show you where to go. I'll give you a full life in the emptiest of places— firm muscles, strong bones. You'll be like a well-watered garden, a gurgling spring that never runs dry. You'll use the old rubble of past lives to build anew, rebuild the foundations from out of your past. You'll be known as those who can fix anything, restore old ruins, rebuild and renovate, make the community livable again.
> —Isaiah 58:9–12, The Message

Wow! As we redig and restore our wells, we bring light and hope to our families and everyone around us. Isaac understood the importance of these wells. I love how his awareness of the favor and promises of God governed his character so that he simply refused to quit. Whatever the opposition, Isaac kept on redigging wells!

When you wake up and realize who sent you, obstacles are nothing more than temporary hindrances. Take back what is yours! The enemy is a thief (John 10:10). He hates it when you realize that you have an inheritance. Redig the wells! They are covered up, but they are still there. Start digging! Let the world see God's hand upon you. The day will come when those who opposed you will say, "We saw clearly that the LORD was with you; so we said, 'There ought to be a sworn agreement between us—between us and you. Let us make a treaty with you'" (Gen. 26:28).

When God's favor is on your life, even your enemies are forced to live at peace with you!

Remember: once you have dug up the wells, you must keep guard over them. Isaac was thirsty for what had been promised to him. He wanted what had been passed down by his father, Abraham. He had to maintain the wells to keep them fresh and flowing. He had to keep the dirt out, just as we have to enter God's presence daily to clean out the dirt that has crept into our lives. Solomon's words encourage us to keep up the maintenance: "Like a muddied spring or a polluted well are the righteous who give way to the wicked" (Prov. 25:26).

Guard the wellspring of your heart! The well was dug for you long ago. Jesus went down to Samaria, to Jacob's well. That is where the Samaritan woman who came to draw water had her thirst quenched forever. Jesus was the well! The enemy tried to cover Him up with dirt. But Satan could not hold back the spring of living water.

Jesus dug the well that never runs dry. Now we need to be well-diggers, too—people who will stand up, grab a shovel, and dig deep. Jesus is calling us today:

> "Let anyone who is thirsty come to me and drink.
> Whoever believes in me, as Scripture has said, rivers
> of living water will flow from within them".
> —JOHN 7:37–38

A MOMENT AT THE WELL

Get the dirt out of the well today! Have a face-off with the enemy and stand up to the opposition so that you can spread out and be blessed! *Dig out!* Pull Jesus up out of the well and into your life, home, and family. No more sitting on the sidelines. Pray and ask God to place in you a warring spirit to defeat the enemy and redig the wells for your family. You must pass on to the next generation a pure, passionate, and undying faith. Pick up a shovel and *keep the wells open!*

Chapter 5

THE POWER OF THE AFTERMATH

As long as the earth endures, seedtime
and harvest, cold and heat, summer and
winter, day and night will never cease.
—GENESIS 8:22

I S IT POSSIBLE to be so transformed by Jesus that the person you used to be doesn't even exist anymore? Is it possible for God to so completely invade your old life that the only remnant of it is a testimony?

What I am talking about is something we rarely discuss. It's what I call the *aftermath*. We are great at sharing our testimonies, but we forget about the cleanup that begins when the old life is over. At every stage, our choices produce an aftermath. Scripture describes it this way: "The sins of some are obvious, reaching the place of judgment ahead of them: the sins of others trail behind them. In the same way, good deeds are obvious, and even those that are not obvious cannot be hidden forever" (1 Tim. 5:24–25).

We must survey what we leave in our wake. Every life leaves a wake behind it. That wake is like a tsunami that rushes the shoreline and sucks everything it can back into the sea. Only that which is grounded and stable remains standing after a wave like that.

What will be left in the wake of your life? Will it be a thirst? A longing for more? A desire to go deeper and press on to a higher calling? Will you pave the way for

God's presence to flood dry and weary souls? Or will your actions leave behind a wake of destruction and pain?

We are living in a dark world that has become perverse and distorted. People are looking for something that is real, true, and of worth. They seek answers to the questions that keep them up nights. They are looking for something to satisfy their deep longing and need for refreshing.

This is where the power of the aftermath comes in. Every generation including the current one lives in the *aftermath*! The word itself is so powerful. Maybe it's because ours is a generation of pleasure-seekers who think little about the consequences of their actions. They are concerned only about what makes them feel good. They don't worry about the ripple effects their choices produce. Whatever makes them feel good becomes their reality and their version of truth.

Your aftermath is important to them. Your life should be a light in our dark world, a wellspring of life that makes others thirsty for God! The Bible says: "You are the salt of the earth. But if the salt loses its saltiness, how can it be made salty again? It is no longer good for anything, except to be thrown out and trampled underfoot" (Matt. 5:13).

We need to stay "salty." How can we cause others to thirst after God's life-giving waters if we are not thirsty and seeking them ourselves? As we travel, my husband and I meet so many people who simply do not want to hear the truth. Why is that? There are many amazing, godly, righteous churches spreading God's truth in its entirety. Yet, the morality of our nation has been diluted because much of the church has been sleeping by the warmth of God's fire.

We need to wake up and stir the coals. We must fan the flames of truth and righteousness until they are a roaring, all-consuming fire once again! We don't need a cozy, comfortable fire but one that will burn away whatever is preventing us from reaching our destiny with God. It's time for the church to get back to telling the truth with love.

We are so worried about offending people that we deceive them into thinking they are OK. The idea that we need to be like the world in order to win the world is sweeping the planet. But if we are just like the world, why would they want to change? We are called to be set apart, to be different. I am not suggesting that we be super-religious or arrogant; but that we live out what we believe and know to be true. We need standards by which to live and raise our children—standards of holiness and integrity and godly principles.

I choose to uphold those standards and tell the truth because I love your soul more than I want to make you feel good. That's not my concept; it's a Jesus idea, and He knows the end from the beginning. He explained two thousand years ago exactly what is happening in America right now:

> God's kingdom is like a farmer who planted good seed in his field. That night, while his hired men were asleep, his enemy sowed thistles all through the wheat and slipped away before dawn. When the first green shoots appeared and the grain began to form, the thistles showed up too.
> —MATTHEW 13:24–26, THE MESSAGE

Grain and thistles grew together as one. No one could tell the difference between the two. The same thing is happening in churches all across America! The truth of God's power and might is being diluted because we lack thirst. We are comfortable and falling asleep in God's presence.

But here is what happens when we Christians fall asleep on our watch: "A little sleep, a little slumber, a little folding of the hands to rest—and poverty will come on you like a thief and scarcity like an armed man" (Prov. 24:33–34).

AFTERMATH AND WATER

As believers in Christ, it is so easy to stop where Jesus began in us. I call this the aftermath—the aftermath of our salvation experience.

So what is *aftermath*? Dictionary.com says it is "something that results or follows from an event, especially one of a disastrous or unfortunate nature; consequence: *'the aftermath of war; the aftermath of the flood.'"*[1]

Some of you deeply understand aftermath, especially the kind that follows your negative experiences. Maybe it's the aftermath of an abortion or physical abuse or rape. Or maybe it's the aftermath of the perversion that invaded our airwaves starting in the 1960s. Some may understand too well the aftermath of choices such as drugs, addictions, or divorce.

Even as we live in the aftermath of salvation, a generation is reaping dirty sheets! The same thing happened in Jeremiah's day:

> We made our bed and now lie in it, all tangled up in the dirty sheets of dishonor. All because we sinned against our GOD, we and our fathers and mothers. From the time we took our first steps, said our first words, we've been rebels, disobeying the voice of our GOD.
>
> —JEREMIAH 3:25, THE MESSAGE

Whether it is of your own making or beyond your control, you experience aftermath. You are not alone in it, however. God sees you and is right there with you. He saw what happened to you and He saw when you messed up. He saw the moment that keeps trying to define who you are. He wants to use it to define you as a conqueror and an overcomer!

Scripture talks about our aftermaths and about God's presence in them:

> Mark well that GOD doesn't miss a move you make; he's aware of every step you take. The shadow of your sin will overtake you; you'll find yourself stumbling all over yourself in the dark. Death is the reward of an undisciplined life; your foolish decisions trap you in a dead end.
>
> —PROVERBS 5:21, THE MESSAGE

We *must* fix the damage that has been done to a generation. We must live in a new aftermath! We *can* lead a generation back to the wellspring and out of the jungle of sin that has entangled them. The battle is raging all around us. It is a battle for the minds of our children and for the next generation of leaders. The ones who have access to the water source are the ones who gain the victory. So we must bring them back to the water that only God can give—the water that keeps them refreshed, hydrated, and energized to fight. It will empower them to stand firm against the enemy's plan to silence the voice of truth!

Let me give you another definition of aftermath that goes back to the word's origins. (It began as an old English term describing what happens after a field is mowed.) The definition says that *aftermath* is a "new growth of grass following one or more mowings, which may be grazed, mowed, or plowed under."[2]

It might be hard to believe, but as a teenager, I had a side job cutting grass. We were not well off, and I was taught to work for what I wanted and needed. I know what a freshly cut field of grass smells like. The fragrance says, "Make way for the new! The old has been cut off; growth can resume." To me it was an exhilarating smell, because it also said that I had done my job.

I found that it was best to cut dry grass in the morning and water it afterward so the water could soak in during the day. The same holds true in my life; it is best to wake up and immediately take my dry and weary soul into the prayer closet. There I can cut away all the junk that so easily entangles me. Then I can soak in the presence of God, which will sustain me throughout our day.

You may be wondering what this has to do with anything. So let me tell you: our nation is losing the smell of fresh-cut grass. We are dry, thirsty, and dehydrated. Where is the smell of the church doing its job? Where is the growth? It's hard to find evidence of the regular "mowing" that encourages new growth in our lives.

We are the richest nation in terms of wealth and freedom, yet we do not give back to God what He has given us. No one in the United States gets arrested for preaching the gospel. No one has to walk several miles barefoot to find clean drinking water. No one has to take a day-long journey to hear God's Word preached. And no one risks his or her life doing so!

You and I are able to enjoy freedom without responsibility. In that environment, we easily become passive. We have water at our fingertips; yet we remain dehydrated. Unless we wake up, the day is coming when our freedom could be taken away. While we sleep, the enemy is planting thistles! It has been going on for a long time. He is trying to cut off our water supply.

Take a good look at this warning from James:

> Now listen, you rich people, weep and wail because of the misery that is coming on you. Your wealth has rotted, and moths have eaten your clothes. Your gold and silver are corroded. Their corrosion will testify

against you and eat your flesh like fire. You have
hoarded wealth in the last days. Look! The wages you
failed to pay the workers who mowed your fields are
crying out against you. The cries of the harvesters
have reached the ears of the Lord Almighty. You have
lived on earth in luxury and self-indulgence. You
have fattened yourselves in the day of slaughter. You
have condemned and murdered the innocent one,
who was not opposing you. Be patient, then, brothers
and sisters, until the Lord's coming. See how the
farmer waits for the land to yield its valuable crop,
patiently waiting for the autumn and spring rains.
You too, be patient and stand firm, because the Lord's
coming is near. Don't grumble against one another,
brothers and sisters, or you will be judged. The Judge
is standing at the door!

—JAMES 5:1–9

Wow, James said there is injustice in the kingdom and
it is time to take responsibility. It is time not only to keep
ourselves purified by the water but also to lead others to it.
We have become selfish in our walk, only thinking of ourselves, never sharing the revelation of freedom with others.
James said that, to see the harvest, we must stand firm and
not give up!

HARVEST AND STORMS

Our salvation is supposed to yield a harvest. Jesus *demands*
that we produce fruit! How can we do that if we are weary,
withered, and lacking in our own lives? The strength that
we show in hard times is what brings glory to God and
directs others to seek the One who gives us strength. It's
easy to praise God when we have money in our pockets
and everyone is healthy. But what about when tragedy
strikes? Do we still believe what the Bible says? Do we still

have faith? Do we still know where to find water for ourselves and others?

We must contend with these questions. Jesus's expectation of harvest places new demands on us. The old ways of living are incompatible with the new creation. In order to produce fruit, there must be pruning. Pruning hurts! Yet the cutting makes new places for fruit to grow. Notice what John's Gospel says about it:

> I am the true vine, and my Father is the gardener. He cuts off every branch in me that bears no fruit, while every branch that does bear fruit he prunes so that it will be even more fruitful. You are already clean because of the word I have spoken to you. Remain in me, as I also remain in you. No branch can bear fruit by itself; it must remain in the vine. Neither can you bear fruit unless you remain in me. I am the vine; you are the branches. If you remain in me and I in you, you will bear much fruit; apart from me you can do nothing. If you do not remain in me, you are like a branch that is thrown away and withers; such branches are picked up, thrown into the fire and burned.
>
> —JOHN 15:1–6

Jesus said He expects us to be different. We are to be connected to Him. Our roots must go deep so His life flows in and through us, empowering us to face anything and everything the enemy throws at us. Just as the towering oak tree remains standing because of its huge underground root system, we are to be like the "tree planted by the water that sends out its roots by the stream. It does not fear when heat comes; its leaves are always green. It has no worries in a year of drought and never fails to bear fruit" (Jer. 17:8).

Unless we spend time at the well being refreshed by Jesus, we become shallow Christians, tossed and blown over by every wind and wave that hits us and threatens our harvest. Instead, we are to be unmovable, unstoppable, unwavering in our faith and our walk with God. When we realize that God never changes, never leaves us, never pulls back, and never wavers, we also realize that our relationship requires ongoing growth and pursuit of Him.

So how deep do our roots go? Too often, we have knowledge of God and His power but lack a personal encounter, that revelation that awakens us and draws us into His presence. We cannot—we must not—be satisfied with having only information rather than revelation about God. We need to push beyond that so we can *experience* His resurrecting power. Let's allow Him to ignite and resurrect that which has lain dormant too long!

I am reminded of when the disciples were in the boat with Jesus and He remained sleeping after a great storm arose. You know how storms arise: The phone rings and you get the doctor's report. Your child's school calls to inform you that there's a problem. Or you hear the words, "I just don't love you anymore."

A storm arose on the sea and the disciples got scared. They woke up Jesus. But notice what He said: "Why are you so afraid? Do you still have no faith?" (Mark 4:40). In other words, "Don't you know Me yet?"

I have learned that, on my worst days, I need to review the long list of things God has done for me. If I can't think of something He did today, I can surely remember something He did yesterday. When I review the list I remember that I am truly blessed and highly favored. I believe that is what Jesus was saying to the disciples: "Why are you so discouraged and in despair. Have I not saved you?"

Even the wind and the waves obey Him. We will quit being afraid when we understand who He really is!

Many times, problems and storms arise when we stop

growing our roots deep into the Living Word. That's when we stop producing fruit. It's not that we don't love the Vine. We do. We are plugged into Him. We gave our hearts to Jesus, and now we love the Vine's long reach. We are also grateful to be connected to others who are attached to the Vine. Yet we are not producing the fruit we ought to produce!

The aftermath of our storms must be fruit production! What did the last storm produce in your life? What did it produce in the lives of those around you? Did it cause you to run to the King or did you lie down and give up?

The aftermath of your salvation should produce fruit even during a drought. Where is the sign that you are different now? The pregnant wife's ever-growing belly is proof that she has been intimate with her husband. There is relationship there. What is growing and showing in your life that proves you have been in relationship with God? If your field has been mowed, where is the smell of fresh grass?

I love what Matthew 7:16 says: "By their fruit you will recognize them. Do people pick grapes from thorn bushes, or figs from thistles?" What kind of fruit are you producing? If you are still forcing those around you to live in the pain of your past, then you have the wrong aftermath! If others are being held hostage to your pain, then *you* are causing their captivity. Your *victim mentality* has made you into the "terrorist."

Owning Your Aftermath

Aftermath should mean maturity, growth, and freedom that are apparent! Here is what that looks like:

- You have an excitement in your spirit.

- You make a decision to stay away from the "old ways."

- Your life screams, "Jesus!" You are a walking billboard for Him.

- You desire discipline and do not seek to ignore it.

- Freedom is more to you than lyrics from a song.

- You obtain power and joy through devotion to Christ and time in His presence.

- In you the world sees someone to emulate, not investigate.

- The anointing on your life speaks louder than your words.

- You use your past not to entrap others but to bring them freedom.

- Your life makes people thirsty for more of Jesus and less of themselves.

This is the aftermath Jesus offers, yet many of us are still living in the wrong aftermath, without the freedom He died to give us. Scripture explains how it happens:

> Don't fool yourself into thinking that you are a listener when you are anything but, letting the Word go in one ear and out the other. Act on what you hear! Those who hear and don't act are like those who glance in the mirror, walk away, and two minutes later have no idea who they are, what they look like.
> —JAMES 1:22–24, THE MESSAGE

Don't forget who you are! The world is full of fun house mirrors that distort your identity; but God's mirror of love (the Bible) reveals the truth of who you are and will show you whether the person you have become is the one He calls

you to be. The Bible declares that we are more than con-
querors and we have overcome. (See Romans 8:37; 1 John
4:4.) The enemy is under our feet. We are children of the
King!

Too many of us read the Word of God as though it were
a fairy tale or one giant parable that doesn't apply to our
lives. But God's Word is living, breathing, and powerful. It
is able to heal, transform, and set free those who are held
captive by the enemy's lies. I know this firsthand, because
through God's power and grace, I continue to taste that
freedom!

What your aftermath looks like depends upon your
relationship with God. In John chapter 5 a man who had
been an invalid for thirty-eight years was beside the pool
of Bethesda with many other infirm people who believed
that angels would come and stir healing waters at the pool.
The sick and lame believed the superstition and hoped
they would be healed.

This day would be different for the lame man John wrote
about. He would go from superstition to experiencing the
true power of God—from believing in man's concept of
refreshing found in a pool to being refreshed by living
water. His miracle began when Jesus arrived. "When Jesus
saw him lying there and learned that he had been in this
condition for a long time, he asked him, 'Do you want to
get well?'" (John 5:6).

This reminds me of the questions God has asked me
on numerous occasions. I believe His deeper question
is: "Do you really want to be free?" Our circumstances,
issues, and struggles become crutches in our lives. Those
crutches become excuses for why we never go to the next
level. They are excuses to remain wounded, offended, or
disadvantaged in some way.

In the account from John's Gospel, the lame man

replied, "I have no one to help me into the pool when the water is stirred. While I am trying to get in, someone else goes down ahead of me" (John 5:7).

Let me stop right here and say, "Stop! *Enough*." Our troubles are not everyone else's fault all the time. We cannot live our lives pointing the finger and saying, "They caused this." Real growth happens when we can replace the pronoun *they* with *I* and declare, "I can do all things through Christ who strengthens me" (Phil. 4:13, NKJV). "I am persuaded that he is able! I am a new creation! Not *they*, but *I* take responsibility for my spiritual growth."

No more excuses! Without the excuses, we might just take responsibility for our own actions and pursue God in earnest. I love what the book of Hebrews says about this:

> In fact, though by this time you ought to be teachers, you need someone to teach you the elementary truths of God's word all over again. You need milk, not solid food! Anyone who lives on milk, being still an infant, is not acquainted with the teaching about righteousness. But solid food is for the mature, who by constant use have trained themselves to distinguish good from evil.
> —Hebrews 5:12–14

It's time to grow up and prepare ourselves by digging deeply into God's Word. We can't rely on everyone else's prayer life or relationship with God. We cannot act like infants waiting for someone to provide spiritual pacifiers every time we get upset, disappointed, or offended. What we need is His Word and time in His presence!

Why wait for other people to hear from God for us? Why are we relying on their prayer life alone? God wants relationship with *us*! He wants to talk to us and give us revelation and wisdom and discernment. He *likes us*! If we want peace, hope, joy, and freedom, we will find them in His presence—and only in His presence.

Spending time in God's presence is my nerve pill! I can be stressed, frazzled, and overwhelmed; but when I turn on worship, get in His presence, praise Him, and go over His many acts of grace on my behalf, every anxiety, fear, and doubt is washed away in the life-giving water that only He provides. I am rehydrated in His presence!

But let's get back to the lame man:

> Jesus said to him, "Get Up! Pick up your mat and walk," At once the man was cured; he picked up his mat and walked. The day on which this took place was a Sabbath, and so the Jewish leaders said to the man who had been healed, "It is the Sabbath; the law forbids you to carry your mat."
> —JOHN 5:8–10

In a moment, in an instant, Jesus healed the man! Jesus said, "Get up and pick up that which has carried you for so long. Pick it up and *you* carry *it* as a testimony of My authority, power, and love. Carry your testimony! Instead of using your crutch as an excuse, push through and carry it as a badge of victory and evidence that you have overcome."

Put down the crutches. Own your aftermath and live the victory!

WHOSE GLORY?

We know it was Jesus who healed the man because the Bible tells us so. But at first, the man didn't know who his healer was. Can you believe it? He never even asked who healed him! When the Jewish leaders asked him what happened he replied:

> The man who made me well said to me, "Pick up
> your mat and walk." So they asked him, "Who is this
> fellow who told you to pick it up and walk?" The man
> who was healed had no idea who it was, for Jesus had
> slipped away into the crowd that was there.
>   —JOHN 5:11–13

Too often, we want the appearance and all the power
of holiness in our lives but we lack the power that comes
through real relationship with God. Isn't it amazing how
we go down to the altar and plead and cry out and wail
before God and then, when He heals and sets us free,
we walk away and leave Him at the altar. We get what
we want and we walk off without noticing that God has
slipped away.

Later, when Jesus found the man at the temple, He said
to him, "'See, you are well again. Stop sinning or something worse may happen to you.' The man went away and
told the Jewish leaders that it was Jesus who had made
him well" (John 5:14).

This is what I believe Jesus was saying to the man: "Your
aftermath is bad. You're running around saying, 'Look at
me!' You don't even realize who touched you."

We go to the altar and have awesome encounters that
change us. Then we get up and brag about who *we* are and
what *we* did. Instead of praising the One who set us free
and placed our feet on solid ground, we say, "Look at me!
Look at what I did!"

How easily we forget the One who washed us clean, gave
us gifts, and delivered us. Can I confess right now how
frustrated I get and how tired I am of hearing "superstar,"
"celebrity" Christians screaming, "Look at *me*. Notice
my giftings, *my* talents, *my* abilities, *my* charisma." They
should be saying, "*He* set me free. I am nothing without

Him! I am saved by grace! Now it is my responsibility to walk in the power of that grace and be different."

It's time to declare: "I once was lost, blind, dirty, and filthy. But through God's redeeming love, grace, and mercy, I am found! I can see again. I have been washed and *made whole*. It is by grace! By grace I am changing and will continue to grow, mature, and be transformed."

What is your aftermath? It should be like a neon sign that screams, "Jesus!" What is trailing behind you in the wake of your life? Pray today and declare, "Aftermath!" The aftermath He prepared for you says, "Life!" The devil's aftermath speaks only of death.

It's time to start over—*today*. Begin anew and decide that when it's all said and done, the greatest thing people can say about you is that you lived a life worthy of Christ's sacrifice for you. Look at what the Bible says about your fresh start:

> Now we look inside, and what we see is that anyone united with the Messiah gets a fresh start, is created new. The old life is gone; a new life burgeons! Look at it! All this comes from the God who settled the relationship between us and him, and then called us to settle our relationships with each other. God put the world square with himself through the Messiah, giving the world a fresh start by offering forgiveness of sins. God has given us the task of telling everyone what he is doing. We're Christ's representatives. God uses us to persuade men and women to drop their differences and enter into God's work of making things right between them. We're speaking for Christ himself now: Become friends with God; he's already a friend with you.
> —2 CORINTHIANS 5:17–20, THE MESSAGE

A MOMENT AT THE WELL

Are you still sitting by the pool, waiting on someone to stir your spiritual waters? Or are you willing to crawl to the One who holds the only healing water through the blood He shed for you? Wherever you are right now, get on your knees and declare that your life will make a difference. Now is the time for your aftermath—as a whole, healed person and a friend of God—to be known. Your life is a billboard! What are you advertising? Don't wait on other people's revelation from God. Stir up your spirit by falling on your knees and entering His presence with thanksgiving. Let your aftermath remind others of fresh-cut grass whose fragrance says, "New growth is on the way." Let the aroma of a healthy, whole life make those who are trailing behind you thirsty for the living water and a real relationship with God.

Chapter 6

IT AIN'T OVER

*Do not gloat over me, my enemy! Though I
have fallen, I will rise. Though I sit in darkness, the LORD will be my light.*

—MICAH 7:8

Have you ever** been through something that
exhausted you and made you want to give up,
lie down, and maybe even die? Have you ever felt so dry
and worn out that words could not express your agony?

Your wordless groanings say it all to God. He hears
your prayers and deep sighs of exhaustion. I believe this
passage says it best:

> Meanwhile, the moment we get tired in the waiting,
> God's Spirit is right alongside helping us along. If
> we don't know how or what to pray, it doesn't matter.
> He does our praying in and for us, making prayer
> out of our wordless sighs, our aching groans. He
> knows us far better than we know ourselves, knows
> our pregnant condition, and keeps us present before
> God. That's why we can be so sure that every detail
> in our lives of love for God is worked into some-
> thing good.
>
> **—ROMANS 8:26–28, THE MESSAGE**

God is not done with you, regardless of what the enemy
has said! God has the power to resurrect what looks dead.
He has the power to refresh your dry and weary soul. He

is able to restore hope where all hope has been lost. It is time to stand firm and fight for your life, for your family, and for your freedom! It's time to realize that God has placed inside you all that is needed to defeat the enemy.

The enemy's goal is clear: to "steal and kill and destroy" (John 10:10). But that is not the end of it. It is time to reclaim what was stolen. Something powerful happens when you realize "it ain't over." That is when it dawns on you that God has a bigger plan. The presence of God overwhelms you, and you regain hope and purpose.

God knows when you are weary, and He calls you to His presence—back to the well. Listen to what He is saying to you:

> Are you tired? Worn out? Burned out on religion? Come to me. Get away with me and you'll recover your life. I'll show you how to take a real rest. Walk with me and work with me—watch how I do it. Learn the unforced rhythms of grace. I won't lay anything heavy or ill-fitting on you. Keep company with me and you'll learn to live freely and lightly.
> —MATTHEW 11:28, THE MESSAGE

I'll never forget the call we received from our son Nate while he was at college. He said that he had terrible pain in his back, which was troubling, because Nate loved football. He had played the game all through junior high and high school. Then he went to college on a football scholarship. Since he was about ten years old, he'd had dreamed of this season in his life. Now the dream had finally come to pass.

At first I was extremely nervous about my boy getting hurt; that is, until I saw Nate plow through several guys on the field and lay them out like pancakes. At that point, I started worrying more about the other players than about my son.

Just before Nate left for college, we found out that he had scoliosis and Scheuermann's disease with kyphosis. The curvature of his spine caused discomfort, but the doctors let Nate decide whether or not he wanted to continue playing football. He decided he would, because it had been his desire for so long. I must admit that I was a bit reluctant and somewhat concerned about the possibility of his getting injured, but I did not want to be an overprotective mother.

After Nate's first semester at college, however, the pain became too severe, and we had the doctor take another look. We listened to all the options and potential scenarios, which included the possibility of paralysis if Nate sustained a hit in just the right area of his back.

The hits he had already taken on the field were taking a toll on his body. It was clear that he had an important decision to make. Nate was now a young man and this was a "grow-up" moment in which his maturity rose to the surface. He listened patiently as the doctor vividly laid out the facts. The room got silent, and the look of loss in Nate's eyes was unmistakable.

As Pat and I saw our son's heart break; our hearts ached for him. Nate's dreams were dashed to the ground. I flashed back to all the football games, late-night workouts, nutritional supplements, and extreme hard work that had brought him to the attainment of his dream, and I was heartbroken for his loss.

Everything Nate had worked so hard for was ripped from his hands in a few short moments and with just a handful of devastating words. There was an instant in which I'm sure he must have felt his world crashing down around him.

The silence seemed to last for an eternity as Pat and I awaited Nate's reaction and prepared to offer him our love and support. Questions swirled through my mind. How could this happen? Why was it happening?

The room seemed to get smaller and smaller as we waited. The enemy, Satan, would have loved to send Nate spiraling into despair—to bring anger, depression, and discouragement into his life and to cause him to give up. But God had better plans than that, and He showed up! The Holy Spirit filled that small room with peace that could only come from a loving Savior. With determination in his eyes, Nate looked up at us and said, "Can I take my guitar back to college? I've decided to quit football. It's not worth taking the chance and being paralyzed. I'm called to change the world, and I don't want to do it from a wheelchair."

For a moment, Pat was stunned by our son's courage; but he regained his composure and said, "Of course."

Pat and I looked at each other in awe of what had just occurred. We expected this to be a devastating experience. After all, it was the end of Nate's dream. But God saw it differently! That moment defined our son, but not in the way the enemy intended. What was meant for Nate's destruction, God used as a launching point for his destiny.

That day, our family realized that we can overcome anything with God! Nate has since graduated college and is married to the most amazing young lady, our daughter-in-love, Adrienne. The two of them are senior high youth pastors at The House with Pastor Glen Berteau in Modesto, California. Nate and Adrienne recently blessed our family with our first grandchild, Jackson Schatzline, who is destined for greatness.

There is something so powerful when, in the midst of adversity, you realize "it ain't over." You sense that God's not done with you, and you understand that He sees the bigger picture. It was certainly a powerful moment in

Nate's life. He didn't give up and become a victim of the enemy. He chose to push through the disappointment and realized that God wasn't done writing his story. Yes, there was a twist in the story line, but it became a great adventure leading to the bigger plan God had in mind!

In the midst of what might have been Nate's worst desert experience, God arranged for a glorious visit to the well of refreshing. There He renewed Nate's hope and gave him a better dream. God had not lost control of the situation, and He wasn't asleep at the wheel. Philippians 1:6 says: "There has never been the slightest doubt in my mind that the God who started this great work in you would keep at it and bring it to a flourishing finish on the very day Christ Jesus appears" (THE MESSAGE).

Nate and his wife are now impacting young people's lives, snatching them out of hopeless situations, and showing them that there is a much better way. That way is Jesus!

WAITING YOUR TURN

So many times in life, we fix our eyes on our circumstances and we lose focus of what God is doing. We develop a "woe is me" mentality that drags us down. It is during these times that we have to stop looking around and start looking up! The Bible says: "Let us fix our eyes on Jesus, the author and perfecter of our faith, who for the joy set before him endured the cross, scorning its shame, and sat down at the right hand of the throne of God" (Heb. 12:2).

I understand that I'm not perfect, but God is. I get it: I am a work in progress. I am walking out this journey day by day. If God hasn't given up on me then why would I give up on myself? However, I must admit that doubt sometimes screams, "It's over!" That is when I need to stop, take a closer look, and trust God!

I absolutely love hearing stories of triumph in very difficult situations. Such is the story of Bethany Hamilton, the
"soul surfer" who lost her arm to a shark attack. Instead
of feeling sorry for herself, Bethany said "Maybe God did
have something bigger planned for me. What we need to
do is trust…and believe.…If I can help others find hope
in God, then that is worth losing my arm for."[1]

God wants you to know that what looks like devastation doesn't have to be a dead end. It *can* be a launching
pad into your destiny.

I want to share a passage of Scripture that tests my
patience over and over again. I am not a very patient
person by nature, but I have learned—despite my whining,
complaining, and murmuring—that God is still in control. If, like me, you have asked more than once, "When is
it my turn for a miracle?" then this passage will speak to
you. It involves a woman who suffered terribly with an ailment that caused bleeding for twelve years. Don't you sup-
pose that she was at the end of her rope and feeling like it
was over for her?

I do. But look at what happened when she touched Jesus:

> When Jesus had again crossed over by boat to
> the other side of the lake, a large crowd gathered
> around him while he was by the lake. Then one
> of the synagogue leaders, named Jairus, came, and
> when he saw Jesus, he fell at his feet. He pleaded
> earnestly with him, "My little daughter is dying.
> Please come and put your hands on her so that she
> will be healed and live." So Jesus went with him.
> A large crowd followed and pressed around him.
> And a woman was there who had been subject to
> bleeding for twelve years. She had suffered a great
> deal under the care of many doctors and had spent
> all she had, yet instead of getting better she grew

worse. When she heard about Jesus, she came up behind him in the crowd and touched his cloak, because she thought, "If I just touch his clothes, I will be healed." Immediately her bleeding stopped and she felt in her body that she was freed from her suffering. At once Jesus realized that power had gone out from him. He turned around in the crowd and asked, "Who touched my clothes?"

—MARK 5:21–30

Jesus was at the shore—multitasking! While He was ministering to people the crowd became a mob pushing against Him from all sides. But one woman "touched" Him. There is a big difference between being pushed and being touched. Jesus recognized the distinction instantly and turned to the crowd to ask whose touch He felt. He was really asking, "Who placed a demand on My anointing? Who touched My prayer life?"

In reading this passage, it is easy to overlook the scene that was interrupted by this woman's miracle. Before she touched Jesus, a man named Jairus had gotten Jesus's attention. I'm sure Jairus did not appreciate being sent to the back of the line. After all, he was a prominent man who, up until this point, probably hadn't liked Jesus! He was a religious leader who understood etiquette and protocol. But at that moment he was in a crisis. Everything changed when his little girl—his precious little angel and gift from God, his relief from a long day and the pull of the world, his pride and joy—got sick. At that moment the weight of everything that matters fell on his shoulders. After all, he was a daddy, and daddies should be able to fix everything. But he could not fix this.

It is amazing to me that little girls have the power to turn grown men into dress-up partners, tea party guests, and their own private prince at a ball. Our daughter, Abby, can interrupt whatever is going on at our house simply by inviting us to one of her themed tea parties. Instantly the world stops and we all head up to her room to see the wonderful fairy tale that awaits (and she never disappoints). Abby is the joy in our home. Her name, *Abigail,* literally means, "the father's joy."[2]

I'm sure it was no different for Jairus and his family. But now his little girl was in trouble. When he left the house her fever was spiking; her breathing had grown shallow; her pale, little body was dehydrating.

In the crisis Jairus found faith! He *believed* and was willing to do anything necessary to save his daughter. So he ran to Jesus, grabbed Him, and said, "Help me!"

I am always taken aback by how we run to Jesus when we are in trouble and beg Him to come home with us. Most other times we say, "See You next Sunday, Jesus." We forget about Him until the next crisis occurs. Yet, He never turns us away. Whatever relationship Jairus did or did not have with Jesus, he found a loving and gracious Savior who was willing to follow him home and heal his daughter!

That is when Jesus felt someone touch Him. The woman had a legitimate need. But imagine what must have gone through Jairus's mind. Just when he thought his turn had come, someone cut in line!

Have you been there? Did you feel like you got lost in the crowd? How many times in your life have you prayed for a miracle only to see everyone around you getting their miracles instead? In those moments, it can feel as though you are spiraling toward your demise. In reality, you are about to find out exactly how deep your faith goes.

When the woman with the issue of blood interrupted Jairus's miracle, he probably thought: "It's all over! We only had a little time—just a short window to receive healing."

But that was when the story got really interesting. It

seems evident to me that Jesus was revealing something more than what seems obvious about the passage. He is teaching us about *true faith*, about pressing in to have an authentic encounter with Him. Remember that the woman had been hemorrhaging for twelve agonizing years. She was considered cursed and wasn't supposed to be out in public. Every week the synagogue rulers, men like Jairus, would come by her house and announce that she was unclean.

Are you getting this? She was declared too dirty to be seen, let alone come to a place of worship before God. Yet she heard the name of Jesus, and she came anyway. Her desperation led her to reach for the hem of His garment, and the healer met her with the mercy and compassion He longs to give to all hurting, broken, and yearning people.

I suspect that Jairus was furious when this "dirty" woman delayed his daughter's miracle. He probably thought, "Is it really that easy to get Jesus distracted and off His game? I mean, come on Jesus, I was here first! I'm a religious leader; I have a title. I do God's work every day. Surely I am more important than this unclean woman!"

But Jesus had a plan. Look at what happened while the dirty woman, a seeming nuisance and hindrance to Jairus's cause, was being healed:

> While Jesus was still speaking, some people came from the house of Jairus, the synagogue leader. "Your daughter is dead," they said. "Why bother the teacher anymore?"
>
> —MARK 5:35

They said, in essence, "It's over, man! Give up. This woman stole your miracle!"

Sometimes the noise around us can keep us from hearing the voice of God and cause our faith to waver.

116   DEHYDRATED

That is when doubt creeps in. In the midst of the chaos, Jairus's daughter had died. The hemorrhaging woman had cost him his miracle!

But Jesus, "overhearing what they said…told the synagogue ruler, 'Don't be afraid; just believe'" (Mark 5:36).

It's time to get your faith back and realize who God is and what He's capable of doing! During hard times and struggles we see God more as our mascot than our Lord. We think His timing must align with our own. We think that our needs are more important than the needs of others.

It is hard to consider someone else's agony when you are dying of thirst yourself. That is why we all need to reach for Jesus's hem. We need to take that big gulp of faith and put Him back on the throne in our lives. It's time to change the atmosphere in our homes and get away from the naysayers and negative thinkers. We need to change the way we respond to God's presence, so we can see the extent of His power!

When Jesus went to Jairus's house, He put out the doubters and chose a select few to witness the miracle:

> He did not let anyone follow him except Peter, James and John the brother of James. When they came to the home of the synagogue leader, Jesus saw a commotion, with people crying and wailing loudly. He went in and said to them, "Why all this commotion and wailing? The child is not dead but asleep." But they laughed at him. After he put them all out, he took the child's father and mother and the disciples who were with him, and went in where the child was.
> —MARK 5:37–40

Everyone else said Jairus's daughter was dead; Jesus said she was sleeping. The mourners and naysayers laughed at Him. (You know you're about to have a breakthrough when everyone is laughing at your level of faith.) These were professional mourners who show up to mourn other people's loss. Sometimes you have to step away from those who habitually feed negativity into your life. Clean out your circle of friends and whatever else is stopping up your faith. "The power of life and death are in the tongue" (Prov. 18:21).

Remember that Jairus's miracle was delayed—or was it? It may seem to be time for your miracle, but it might not be your turn yet. I believe the delay Jairus endured served a purpose: Jairus's faith was activated by seeing someone else get healed and set free. Though he might not have realized it and might have been frustrated by it, Jairus needed to see that bleeding woman made whole. He needed to see God redeem someone whom society had forgotten. If God would have mercy on her then surely He would show the same kindness to Jairus.

When Jairus's turn came, Jesus kicked out everyone who lacked faith. Then He approached the little girl:

> [Jesus] took her by the hand and said to her, "*Talitha koum!*" (which means, "Little girl, I say to you, get up!"). Immediately the girl stood up and began to walk around (she was twelve years old). At this they were completely astonished. He gave strict orders not to let anyone know about this, and told them to give her something to eat.
>
> —Mark 5:41–43

Jesus told them to give the miracle something to eat! She was dehydrated and needed refreshment. When Jesus "resurrects" you, you have to feed your faith and testify of His goodness! It's time to stand up and declare, "It ain't over!"

DON'T BET AGAINST GOD!

Scripture gives many examples of those who kept the faith despite the battle. Hebrews chapter 11 is the Bible's "hall of fame" for such victors. These are the people who refused to quit. They realized (against all odds), that "it ain't over" just because it *looks* over.

We can have similar testimonies. In fact, because of the cross, we ought to have even greater ones! We only need to remember who God is and how completely He can be trusted. Paul reminded the Corinthians of these very things:

> Just think—you don't need a thing, you've got it all! All God's gifts are right in front of you as you wait expectantly for our Master Jesus to arrive on the scene for the Finale. And not only that, but God himself is right alongside to keep you steady and on track until things are all wrapped up by Jesus. God, who got you started in this spiritual adventure, shares with us the life of his Son and our Master Jesus. He will never give up on you. Never forget that.
> —1 CORINTHIANS 1:7–9, THE MESSAGE

This is your hour to rise up with power and authority. It's time to declare freedom over your life and the lives of your family members. It's time to stand up and serve notice that the enemy cannot have your marriage or your kids!

For those of you who feel like you're at the end, your time is up, and you have been forgotten or misplaced—it ain't over! In fact, for the body of Christ, things are just beginning! Jesus has not given up on us. His power is all that we need! Nothing is too hard for our God.

If you are still tempted to doubt Him, allow me to make some suggestions:

- Don't tell Noah it's over and there's no such thing as rain or an ark.

- Don't tell Moses it's over as the bush burns and his future is marked by God.

- Don't tell Esther it's over as she marches into the king's chamber to save her people.

- Don't tell Ruth it's over as she gleans in the field of Boaz—her redeemer—and enters the lineage of Christ.

- Don't tell David it's over as Goliath insults God's people and David reaches for one smooth stone.

- Don't tell Nehemiah it's over as he rebuilds the wall in record time.

Here are some more history-makers whose minds you would not have changed:

- Don't tell Christopher Columbus there is no new world.

- Don't tell the founding fathers we can't govern ourselves.

- Don't tell Abraham Lincoln all men aren't created equal.

- Don't tell Thomas Edison there's no such thing as a lightbulb.

- Don't tell Rosa Parks she can't sit in the front of the bus.

- Don't tell Dr. Martin Luther King Jr. that his dream won't come true.

- Don't tell Nelson Mandela that South Africa can't be free from apartheid; and especially don't do it as he quotes author Marianne Williamson:

Our deepest fear is not that we are inadequate. Our deepest fear is that we are powerful beyond measure. It is our light, not our darkness that most frightens us. We ask ourselves, "Who am I to be brilliant, gorgeous, talented, fabulous?" Actually, who are you not to be? You are a child of God. Your playing small does not serve the world. There is nothing enlightened about shrinking so that other people won't feel insecure around you. We are all meant to shine, as children do. We were born to make manifest the glory of God that is within us. It's not just in some of us; it's in everyone. And as we let our own light shine, we unconsciously give other people permission to do the same. As we are liberated from our own fear, our presence automatically liberates others.[3]

Don't tell my husband and me that we can't go to a distant land, adopt our precious daughter, and make our family complete.

History is full of people who should have thought it was over but held on to faith anyway. Greatest among them was Jesus!

Do you see what this means—all these pioneers who blazed the way, all these veterans cheering us on? It means we'd better get on with it. Strip down, start running—and never quit! No extra spiritual fat, no parasitic sins. Keep your eyes on Jesus, who both began and finished this race we're in. Study how he did it. Because he never lost sight of where he was headed—that exhilarating finish in and with God— he could put up with anything along the way: cross,

shame, whatever. And now he's there, in the place
of honor, right alongside God. When you find yourselves flagging in your faith, go over that story again,
item by item, that long litany of hostility he plowed
through. That will shoot adrenaline into your souls!
—HEBREWS 12:1–3, THE MESSAGE

C. S. Lewis said, "I pray because I can't help myself. I
pray because I'm helpless. I pray because the need flows
out of me all the time—waking and sleeping. It does not
change God—it changes me."[4] God knows you want to
give up. He sees you dangling between destiny and cir-
cumstance. But God hasn't forgotten you. He is working it
out for your good. He loves you! The Bible says: "Wake up!
Strengthen what remains and is about to die, for I have
not found your deeds complete in the sight of my God"
(Rev. 3:2, NAS).

In other words, God's not done with you. It's not over!
When gold goes through the fire, it is "proven" and comes
out pure (1 Pet. 1:7). God will display your faith, not your
gold, as proof of His victory.

Are you dehydrated? It's time to head back to the well.
You need living water every day. Every day you must go
to the place of refreshment—His presence. There you will
regain your strength and find the water that sustains and
strengthens you to face every obstacle the enemy throws
your way. Stay spiritually hydrated and you will stay in
the fight and not quit. He is at the well waiting to refresh
you today.

A MOMENT AT THE WELL

As you finish this chapter, receive the authority to trample
on the enemy and defeat him in every area of your life. I
challenge you to declare, "It ain't over!" to the areas that
seem dead, dry, and defeated. Walk through your house

and speak life over them. Then watch what God does in and through you! Declare that the enemy has no authority over your life or your family. Relinquish all control to God. Declare victory and freedom over your household, your marriage, your children, your finances, and your health. Declare that breakthrough is coming and what you see in the natural is not the final answer. Determine that the enemy will not bully you. God is on the throne!

It *ain't* over!

Chapter 7

HOPE FLOATS

Hope does not put us to shame, because God's
love has been poured out into our hearts through
the Holy Spirit, who has been given to us.

—ROMANS 5:5

I'M SINKING, GOD! I can't even see the shore! I'm drowning in a sea of hopelessness and I'm not sure I have the strength to survive!" Those are the words I cried one miraculous morning when I felt lost at sea and unable to find my way out of despair.

Mental confusion—the loss of orientation and the inability to think through your options—is one of the surest signs of severe dehydration. When you cannot think rationally or see clearly, hopelessness sets in. As you grasp frantically for some way to cling to life, the hope drains out of your soul.

Hopelessness is running rampant in our world. This generation is what I call the "medicated generation" because the realities and stresses of everyday life have left so many feeling defeated, depressed, and walking in despair. The facts of life are too painful to manage so we dull our senses in order to survive.

Fasten your seat belt, because I'm about to be even more real and transparent with you than I have been so far. I'm going to explain why you don't have to sink into the abyss of hopelessness. You don't have to live in despair. There is hope for the hopeless and freedom from despair. You might feel like you are sinking, but hope will rise to the surface as surely as a cork will rise from under the sea.

The Bible says: "Hope deferred makes the heart sick, but a longing fulfilled is a tree of life" (Prov. 13:12). The enemy's number one goal is to keep us so beaten down that we lose all strength. Satan wants to keep us confused and lost so that we cannot find the living water that leads us back to freedom.

God has called us to walk in freedom and power. He has called us to dream big dreams. But life can get tough—so tough that we become weary, drained, and desperate for refreshing.

HOPE BEYOND DESPAIR

The Bible says that the "thief comes only to steal and kill and destroy" (John 10:10, NAS). The enemy wants what he didn't create, what he didn't work for and what he didn't die for! But look at what Jesus went on to say in the same verse: "I came that they [you] may have life, and have it abundantly."

The Greek word translated "life" in this verse is *zoe,* which speaks to vitality and "the absolute fullness of life."[1] The Greek word for "abundantly" is *perissos,* meaning "over and above, more than is necessary."[2]

While the enemy is bent on our destruction and death, Jesus comes with a surge of fresh life that is more than what is necessary to sustain us and bring us out of our despair. He gives us more life than we deserve!

Everyone goes through seasons of despair and hopelessness caused by physical issues and other circumstances. I have been through some of those seasons and have learned that our spiritual roots are there for a reason. Roots speak of the future. The dead of winter always gives way to new life in the spring. Some things on the surface have to die in order for new life to spring forth, as long as the roots hold.

Have you noticed that the rainbow doesn't appear until the storm is over? At every major crossroads in mine and Pat's life, God has shown us a rainbow. In the midst of what otherwise seemed like chaos, God used those rainbows to show us that His promises for us are still "yes and amen" (1 Cor. 1:20). God is still in control. "We wait in hope for the LORD; he is our help and our shield" (Ps. 33:20).

I have found that what we go through is not as important as who we run to for help. At times I have not felt very godly; there did not seem to be much hope in waiting on the promises God had given me. The dreams He placed in my heart seemed too far out of my reach and I lacked the strength to attain them.

Some of you know what I am talking about. Some of you have let certain dreams die. Some promises have gone unfulfilled. Maybe you feel as though a dark cloud has settled over you and you can't see through the fog to find your way out. But it is time to dream again! God is the God of the dark times! You are never alone. God is always in the dark places with you, and He can see in the dark.

At times in my life I have dealt with deep despair and discouragement and even depression. It's easy to sink into despair when you want to be the one in control. Letting go seems so difficult because it requires total surrender to God. Surrender is not easy for slight control freaks like me! But I have learned that depression and despair don't give exceptions to control freaks or anyone else. Depression and despair are equal-opportunity offenders; they affect the rich and poor, the famous and the not-so-well-known.

After the birth of my son I dealt with what we now call postpartum depression. There were times when I felt so ashamed *not* to be overflowing with joy in the months following Nate's birth. Of course I was thrilled with my precious gift and with being a new mommy. Yet there was an underlying sadness that I could not put my finger on. I put on a good face for everyone around me, but inside I felt empty, hopeless, and lost, for no apparent reason.

For months I struggled in silence, wondering if I would ever be joyful again. Finally I decided that I had had enough. I got down on my knees, crawled into my prayer closet, and cried out to the only one who had the power to set me free. He was the only one I knew would not judge or condemn me in my despair. He alone could breathe new life and joy and strength—and yes, even *hope*—back into my life.

I spoke Scripture over my life and I warred in the spirit over my mind and my heart. I'm sure that wonderful medicines were available to help me through my difficulty, but because it was taboo and postpartum depression was not widely discussed back then, I was afraid to admit that I was struggling and I feared being labeled "depressed." After all, I was a Christian and I was in ministry. I thought I was supposed to be perfect and have it all together. Wow! Was I ever wrong.

There comes a point when you are sick and tired of being beat up by the devil. You realize who the King of kings is and you understand the scripture that says, "Greater is he that is in you, than he that is in the world" (1 John 4:4, KJV).

That's where I was. So I pressed into God's throne room every day and filled my mind and heart with His Word. I gained an understanding of who God really is and how much He loves me and wants me to be free. I realized that without Him, I could do nothing; but I was reminded that "I can do all things through Christ which strengtheneth me" (Phil. 4:13, KJV). Not only did Christ want me to survive—He wanted me to overcome and defeat the enemy's plan to destroy me.

Another scripture became life to me: "Now faith is confidence in what we hope for and assurance about what we do not see" (Heb. 11:1). It was by no means an easy journey, but in time I saw hope rising in the distance. God delivered me and restored my joy and zest for life. He reminded me that He is always with me and will never leave me. I clung to that hope and refused to let go. Each and every day I moved closer to freedom.

LET THERE BE!

I absolutely believe in God's ordained plan for your life. Everything you go through serves a purpose and should make you stronger. With every victory comes new freedom, strength, and understanding of God's love and mercy and grace. During the ten years following my son's birth, I would be required to draw from that strength and hold on to that hope once again as I embarked on a journey of trust with my Savior.

I share my story to show you that God always reaches into the depths of the dark abyss and brings forth life beyond anything you can imagine. That is exactly what He did when He created the earth and all that came out of the darkness!

> In the beginning God created the heavens and the earth. Now the earth was formless and empty, darkness was over the surface of the deep, and the Spirit of God was hovering over the waters. And God said, "Let there be light," and there was light. God saw that the light was good, and he separated the light from the darkness.
>
> —GENESIS 1:1–4

Notice that the Spirit of God hovered over the waters. God hovered over you before you knew Him. He was planning and dreaming dreams for you. When an airplane prepares to land, it circles the airport. The pilot is waiting for the control tower to clear the aircraft for landing. I have been in that hover mode many times; it can be very frustrating to know you are so close to your destination, yet so far from touching down. Finally, when it is safe to land, the pilot gets the OK from the tower.

That is what God is doing: He is hovering over you and making sure all the junk is out of the way. When He is certain your "runway" is cleared and you are ready to land safely, He will OK the next leg of your journey.

Notice what Genesis 1:1 says: "the earth was formless and empty." These are the conditions in which God works! If He can create the universe out of nothing, He can bring you out of anything! You might feel like you are drowning in the abyss of darkness, but God pulled light from the darkness when He created the world. Now, He is reaching inside you, pulling the light from within and drawing it out to the surface. The light is there; you just haven't seen it yet.

During the process of being brought out of despair, you must realize that certain attitudes and emotions can delay your miracle and destroy your destiny. Offense, anger, bitterness, and fear can derail your freedom and prevent your getting to the next level. Be patient with the process. When you feel as though a dark cloud hangs over you and you are lost in the fog, you are exactly where the creation once was!

God has not forgotten you or decided that you don't matter. He is moving the junk out of the way so you can land in your destiny. Take heart! God waits until there is *nothing* left. Then He says, "Let there be!" I pray that this is your "Let There Be Day" of freedom, joy, power, and authority—a day to realize that hope floats!

DESPAIR AND DELIVERANCE

BEFORE WE CONTINUE on the subject of hope, let's look into the workings of despair. What is it? According to one definition, despair means: "To lose hope: [for example] *despaired of reaching shore safely....* To be overcome by a sense of futility or defeat."[3]

Have you ever felt that way? Was it a struggle to pull yourself out of bed each morning? Was it hard to imagine an end to your agony? Then you can relate to what the psalmist said: "From my youth I have suffered and been close to death; I have borne your terrors and am in despair" (Ps. 88:15).

Solomon understood such feelings and described their terrible effects:

> So I hated life, because the work that is done under the sun was grievous to me. All of it is meaningless, a chasing after the wind. I hated all the things I had toiled for under the sun, because I must leave them to the one who comes after me.
>
> —ECCLESIASTES 2:17–18

Solomon was depressed and in despair, but he was also self-absorbed. He seemed unable to see beyond himself and his own circumstances to the bigger picture. It is crucial for us to realize that *it's not all about us!* We get overwhelmed in our own pits of despair when we spend our lives looking through a microscope and not telescopes. It's time to see the lost and hurting around us so we can recognize the blessings in our own lives.

You have a purpose that reaches far beyond your own issues. But have you ever felt like Solomon did, as though nothing you do ever works out? The spirit of despair comes when you feel unable to control your circumstances.

Parents lose hope when their children stray and make bad decisions. Married couples lose hope when they face hard times relationally. Providers lose hope when the economy falters and jobs become scarce.

God is not unaware or limited by these struggles. Look at what He stands ready to do:

> He has sent me to bind up the brokenhearted, to proclaim freedom for the captives and release from darkness for the prisoners, to proclaim the year of the LORD's favor and the day of vengeance of our God, to comfort all who mourn, and to provide for those who grieve in Zion—to bestow on them a crown of beauty instead of ashes, the oil of joy instead of mourning, and a garment of praise instead of a spirit of despair. They will be called oaks of righteousness, a planning of the LORD for the display of his splendor.
> —ISAIAH 61:1–3

This is your day to declare victory over despair! You are called to walk in victory! God took what was hidden and brought it into the light. Then He said "It is good!" When God gets done with you, He voices His approval. He likes what He has made. He made you in His own image (Gen. 1:26) and is pleased with you. No matter how messed up your life may be, He takes it and forms something new out of its "nothingness." He recreates us in ways that reveal who we belong to and show us how faithful He is. Paul explained it this way:

> But we have this treasure in jars of clay to show that this all-surpassing power is from God and not from us. We are hard pressed on every side, but not crushed; perplexed, but not in despair; persecuted, but not abandoned; struck down, but not destroyed.
> —2 CORINTHIANS 4:7–9

Nevertheless, there are days and seasons in which these jars of clay experience despair. I remember a certain day— it was just another school morning and I was preparing breakfast for my son. However, this morning was different. I felt the enemy's claws of discouragement and despair trying to take hold of my life again. It just so happened that Pat was not home. He was in Tennessee to speak at a church there.

Seven long years had passed since he and I had started trying to conceive again. Nate was in the third grade and was a total joy and blessing in our lives. He has always been our miracle, and I knew we had the perfect family. Yet something was missing. I longed to have at least one more child. I knew God had promised me that I would, but it just wasn't happening. I had dreams and visions of holding my second child, but one disappointment after another had taken a toll on me.

Many friends, loved ones, and great leaders had prophesied that we would hold another child. Others told me that I should just be happy to have one child. They meant well, but when God places a desire and a promise in your heart, you cannot suppress it no matter how hard you try.

I have to admit that on this particular morning, I felt angry, cheated, and forgotten, as though I was being robbed of the blessing that God had for me and my family. I was not satisfied with settling or giving up. As I prepared to take Nate to school, I murmured and complained under my breath: "Why me, God? Why won't You give me a second child? I'm a good mother. I'm a loving mother. Why me?"

These questions rolled over and over in my head, all the way to school and throughout the drive home. Have you ever gotten mad and poured out your heart to God? Have you ever told God what He should do for you?

I did it all that day. Basically, I was throwing myself a

pity party, declaring, "Woe is me. Poor, pitiful me!" At
one point, I lifted my fist to heaven and asked, "Where are
You? Don't You care about me, God?" (As if that would
move God or make Him give me my way!)

Around that time I reached home and pulled into the
garage. I honestly do not know how I got home safely that
day, as I was preoccupied with my pity party for one. As I
turned off the car, I remained in the driver's seat and wept
for the loss of my dream. I screamed, "I give up! I can't do
this anymore."

Finally, I let it go! Then something miraculous happened: As I sobbed, I heard God speak to me. It was not
an audible voice, but the voice I heard in my spirit was
clearer than anything I had ever heard since my seventh-
grade experience on the concrete bench. The same loving
God who sat beside me when I was thirteen now joined
me in the garage and in my hopelessness.

That's the thing about God—He will meet you *any-
where* and He will speak to you! Sometimes hearing His
voice happens only when we get to the end of ourselves
and let go of all control. Then finally, amid all the noise
around us, He speaks.

I had definitely come to the end of myself, and these are
the words I heard Him say: "Karen—good! Finally, I can
do a work in your life. Wake up! You're not alone. I need
you to survive."

That got my attention. I don't know about you, but I am
stubborn. God speaks to me in a very loving, but matter-
of-fact way to get my attention. What my loving Father
said next changed the very core of my being. He asked,
"If you were on a ship in the middle of the ocean and that
ship was sinking, what would keep you alive?"

To be honest, the question caught me off guard. I
sat almost frustrated for a few minutes; the question

didn't seem to relate to what I was going through. Then I responded with this statement: "God, on this particular day, I don't know if I want to survive. But wait—the only thing that would keep me alive on that sinking ship, would be my knowing that Nate was on the ship, too. I would definitely stay alive to ensure his safety."

God spoke to my heart, and said, "Exactly, Karen. Not everything is about you. Sometimes the despair or crises you endure are for others who need to see you survive so they will have the strength to survive themselves. Sometimes in your despair, what you really need is to rescue someone else. In your despair, *rescue!*"

I continued weeping, but no longer out of self-pity. It was the revelation that, all this time, God had been taking me on a journey in order to change me. It had been about my waking up to the fact that everything is not about me; it is about those to whom I am called. There was a greater purpose, a greater vision, a greater hope.

Still sitting in the car, I had a vision in which a map appeared before me—a map of China. I stared at it in wonder and heard God say, "There is your daughter! There is your miracle. She is waiting on you, but you weren't ready until now."

This wasn't even about my dreams and desires. This was about Abby and how God had been writing her story and making plans for her life since before she was born. My trial was about her destiny! Somehow, in the story and song of her life, I was transformed forever. In one of the driest seasons of my life, as I wept in my car, the rain of God's presence fell on me, like droplets refreshing my parched spirit.

Once I regained my composure, I ran inside and called Pat. As I shared with him what God had told me, I could tell he was tearing up. He told me that God had spoken to him a few months earlier and showed him that we were to adopt. God had instructed him not to say anything, because I needed an encounter in which God would tell me Himself.

Even more amazing was the fact that the pastor for whom Pat was ministering had picked him up and taken him to lunch along with the pastor's wife and precious daughter. They had recently adopted the child from China! How beautiful and miraculous are the plans God lays out for us. How amazing are the steps He has ordered for us.

The pastor referred us to the amazing adoption agency that he and his wife had worked with: Children of the World, in Fairhope, Alabama. We immediately began the journey to bring home our beautiful daughter, Abigail Xiu He Schatzline.

God had a bigger and better plan than I realized. He has *amazing* plans for Abby, and I am so grateful to be her mother and be given the opportunity to be a part of it all. People often approach me and say how blessed Abby is that we went to China and rescued her. I embrace the opportunity to correct them and say, "No. I am blessed that Abby rescued me."

I needed to be rescued! When I was in despair, I was just surviving. I felt confounded, as though living with no answers. Being confounded is an aspect of despair that keeps us in survival mode. But we are not called to survive. We are to be overcomers, victorious and walking in the light of Christ.

In my "garage encounter" with God, I went from crying out, "My God, I cry out by day, but you do not answer, by night, but I find no rest" (Ps. 22:2), to standing up and declaring, "Now may the God of hope fill you with all joy and peace in believing so that you will abound in hope by the power of the Holy Spirit" (Rom. 15:13, NAS).

God never disappoints or lets us down. His plans might unfold differently than we expect them to, but praise God! His plans are always far better than anything we could imagine. He is the One who brings us out—our deliverer!

SHAKE OFF THE DIRT

God delivers, but we have to *choose* to be victors rather than victims! Part of choosing to be a victor in the midst of your circumstances is being able to recognize the workings of despair. It is important to know how despair begins. Consider the following list. Are any of these "conditions" causing you to despair?

- Feeling as though you do not matter
- Feeling that you can't accomplish anything and arc just spinning your wheels
- Believing that you work *for* God and not *with* God (works instead of a relationship)
- Believing that what others say and do can diminish your worth or value
- Believing your dreams are impossible or dead
- Thinking that every bad thing that *can* happen *does* happen
- Walking in the fear of the unknown
- Feeling that your circumstances are not meeting up to your expectations

I want you to know that the enemy is an embezzler! He takes what does not belong to him. It's time for your *hope* to *float*! You are not called to live under oppressive spirits. You are called to live under the power of Almighty God!

That should remind you of Jesus carrying His cross for your sake, and of the lame man carrying what once carried him. (See Luke 5:18–25.)

You were meant to live under God's power, peace, joy, purpose, and freedom! "There is one body and one Spirit, just as you were called to one hope when you were called; one Lord, one faith, one baptism; one God and Father of all, who is over all and through all and in all" (Eph. 4:4–6).

You flourish when you live under God's power and authority! You have victory over whatever the enemy intended to kill you with. I am reminded of the story of the mule that fell into an old abandoned well. The owner of the mule was an old farmer. He decided to throw dirt in the well to bury the mule and end its misery. Instead, the mule shook off every shovelful of dirt and stomped on it. Eventually, the mule walked out of the well! What was meant to bury him built a pathway out of the pit.

It's time to come out of your pit! You are called to be under God's love and strength. The level of your strength is determined by whom you choose to walk under. It reminds me of one of our vacations at the beach when our son Nate was a little boy. He ran along the shore with a beach towel tied around his neck like a superhero's cape. When he saw Pat's shadow surrounding him, he yelled, "Look Daddy! I'm in your shadow."

We are to walk under the shadow of the Almighty! The Bible says: "He who dwells in the secret place of the Most High shall abide under the shadow of the Almighty" (Ps. 91:1, NKJV).

We need hope. People are always looking for hope. Merriam-Webster states that *hope* is "to wish for something with expectation of its fulfillment...to have confidence; trust."[4] I have found that Jesus is my only hope. People will let you down. Positions and titles will let you down. Dreams will let you down. But Jesus will never let you down! God says that hope is waiting for you. Your miracle and your blessing are waiting for you. My miracle was waiting for me in China, but I had to walk out my faith, pursuing the hope and joy set before me.

God wants to restore your life! You will never be sorry for putting your hope in Him!

> No one who hopes in you will ever be put to shame, but shame will come on those who are treacherous without cause. Show me your ways, LORD, teach me your paths. Guide me in your truth and teach me, for you are God my Savior, and my hope is in you all day long.
> —PSALM 25:3-5

You are called to one hope and one power! Your hope is in His resurrection! He died so that you might live! "Praise be to the God and Father of our Lord Jesus Christ! In his great mercy he has given us new birth into a living hope through the resurrection of Jesus Christ from the dead, and into an inheritance that can never perish, spoil or fade" (1 Pet. 1:3-4).

If you want your hope to float, change the way you wake up each day. Shake off the dirt! Wage war on the enemy and take back your mind and your heart. Realize that your life is worthy of hope, joy, and strength. There are people who need to see you break free in order for their faith to be activated. Others will be strengthened by your freedom! Your own family needs to see you get free.

Develop daily reminders of hope. Realize that you are not the only one who is under attack. "Be alert and of sober mind. Your enemy the devil prowls around like a roaring lion looking for someone to devour. Resist him, standing firm in the faith, because you know that the family of believers throughout the world is undergoing the same kind of sufferings" (1 Pet. 5:8–9).

Realize that you have a choice: to walk in victory or embrace defeat. You get to make this choice every day that you wake up in your flesh body. *Joy is a choice*—a place you choose to reside. Remind yourself that you cannot change lives for God's glory while walking in defeat. Let your daily mission be to search for joy, power, and authority in God. Ask God for fresh vision, ideas, and dreams. Remember that you are called to a greater purpose, not just for yourself but for those you are called to rescue. You have been chosen to direct them to the One who can heal, restore, and raise them out of the pit.

A MOMENT AT THE WELL

Climb out of the abyss today! Pray that your heart would be open to receive hope, joy, and freedom. Let hope arise in you! Pray that through your example (your testimony) your family will have the strength and courage to arise and walk out the life that God has called them to live. Pray today that God will strengthen you to be a voice of life to everyone with whom you come in contact. Hope is contagious! It's time for hope to float up from your pit and become a living well of refreshing waters. Your family deserves a free *you*! Spread the hope and freedom that only Christ can give.

Chapter 8

GET YOUR PRAISE ON

As they began to sing and praise, the LORD set ambushes
against the men of Ammon and Moab and Mount Seir
who were invading Judah, and they were defeated.
—2 CHRONICLES 20:22

P RAISE WAS RESTORED at the well when the Samaritan woman met the Messiah (John 4). It not only restored her life, but, also the understanding of whom we are called to worship, and how. As Jesus said: "A time is coming and has now come when the true worshippers will worship the Father in the Spirit and in truth, for they are the kind of worshippers the Father seeks" (v. 23).

Your thirst is quenched when you worship and praise in truth. Jesus cried out, "If anyone thirsts, let him come to me and drink. Rivers of living water will brim and spill out of the depths of anyone who believes in me this way, just as the Scripture says" (John 7:37–38, THE MESSAGE).

Jesus wants you to drink from the well that never runs dry; but He also wants you to *become* a living well that leads others to drink and leave their thirst behind. Jesus put the well in us so that we would lead people to drink.

This chapter is for those who have decided that Jesus is the living well and they are going to live according to God's Word regardless of what circumstances they face or what war the enemy brings. It is also for those who realize that "it ain't over" and hope does indeed rise above our circumstances.

PRAISE AND POWER

It is so important to understand that even if you do not understand where life has landed you at this moment, whatever struggle you are facing will be worth it in the end. You can live out your dreams in spite of what you have to walk through to do it.

If your life feels more like an empty pit than a life-giving well; if your river is not flowing as it should; it's time to *do something*. When your river is dammed up, bring out the dynamite! It will unstop and unclog your river so that joy can flow freely again. That dynamite is *praise*! Praise demolishes the work of the enemy and sends confusion into his camp. What better way is there to open the dam than to use spiritual dynamite!

Jesus said that His people would be endued "with power from on high" (Luke 24:49).[1] The Greek word for "power" is *dunamis*, from which we get the word *dynamite*.[2] Dynamite! Do you see what God has given you? He said He gave you power, or dynamite to break open the dam in your life! And when you praise Him, it proves that you know where your strength comes from.

This is how you keep from becoming dry and dehydrated: begin your day with praise and end it the same way. God has placed dreams, visions, and purpose in your life. The enemy will do anything and everything he can to keep them from being fulfilled. Your praise releases freedom in your spirit and opens the windows of heaven. Instead of focusing on yourself and your problems (and becoming self-centered and prideful), praise forces your attention back to God, the very source of dunamis.

Praise is the key to walking out a life of faith and freedom. Whenever your faith is at an all-time high, you will see that praise is present. Praise and thankfulness are connected. Notice what Scripture says: "So then, just as you received Christ Jesus as Lord, continue to live your lives in him, rooted and built up in him, strengthened in the faith as you were taught, and overflowing with thankfulness" (Col. 2:6–7).

Our praise is acknowledgment that we can do nothing in ourselves, but with God, we can do anything. Praise builds us up spiritually and tears down walls of fear and doubt. Nehemiah 8:10 declares that the "joy of the Lord is your strength"! Joshua understood this when he led the Israelites around the city of Jericho for the seventh time and ordered, "Shout! For the Lord has given you the city!"

If you want certain walls to crumble in your life or you need strongholds to come down, then I say, "It's time to *praise!*" It's time to declare freedom in your life and see past yourself and your current situation. You might feel as though life has dealt you a bad hand. It might seem like you just can't get past today. But you can! Consider the apostle Paul. I would say that he faced more adversity than most of us will ever experience. He was flogged, stoned, shipwrecked, imprisoned, and more. Yet here's what Paul said in the midst of his suffering:

> So we're not giving up. How could we! Even though on the outside it often looks like things are falling apart on us, on the inside, where God is making new life, not a day goes by without his unfolding grace. These hard times are small potatoes compared to the coming good times, the lavish celebration prepared for us. There's far more here than meets the eye. The things we see now are here today, gone tomorrow. But the things we can't see now will last forever.
> —2 Corinthians 4:16–18, The Message

You see, what you are going through today is nothing compared to the joy of spending eternity with Christ. Praise will push you past your fleshly desert into a spirit realm of refreshing where you can see clearly how much God has done for you. I told you earlier that God's presence is my nerve pill. Well, praise and worship are, too! When I get overwhelmed and anxiety tries to overtake me, I turn up the worship and I praise Him. Soon, everything that had me down is swallowed up in the greatness of my God!

Paul and Silas understood praise. When they were locked in the dungeon for doing the will of God, they turned up their praise:

> Along about midnight, Paul and Silas were at prayer and singing a robust hymn to God. The other prisoners couldn't believe their ears. Then, without warning, a huge earthquake! The jailhouse tottered, every door flew open, all the prisoners were loose.
> —ACTS 16:25–26, THE MESSAGE

The enemy tries to lock us up in dungeons of despair when we faithfully run the race we were called to run. Satan doesn't understand that when he slams the prison door shut, he sets the stage for a prison break that glorifies God!

Do you see what happened when Paul and Silas praised Him? Not only did their praise reach heaven and set them free, but it set free all of the other prisoners, too.

Your praise affects you and those around you. It gets the attention of God and stirs His heart toward compassion. It releases the captives and sets them free. God inhabits the praises of His people (Ps. 22:3). But He is also the living water, and He inhabits *us*. Because He lives in us, we are wells that should never run dry.

DREAMS, PRAISE, AND THE PIT

I LOVE TO HEAR stories about crazy dreamers, most of whom are crazy worshippers, too. They are my favorite people—the ones who never live *where they are* but *where they are going.* Joseph was a crazy dreamer in the Bible— one of many I want to meet when I get to heaven. He remained in a continual state of living for what God had promised, regardless of how things looked in the natural.

Not everyone appreciated Joseph's faith and determination. "'Here comes that dreamer!' [his brothers] said to each other. 'Come now, let's kill him and throw him into one of these cisterns and say that a ferocious animal devoured him. Then we'll see what comes of his dreams'" (Gen. 37:19–20).

Wow! "Here comes that dreamer. Let's kill him!" That is exactly what the devil says when he sees you coming with all your God dreams inside you. It sends him into a fury. Joseph's brothers hated him and his dreams. His oldest brother tried to rein them in and keep Joseph alive:

> When Reuben heard this, he tried to rescue him from their hands. "Let's not take his life," he said. "Don't shed any blood. Throw him into this cistern [well] here in the desert, but don't lay a hand on him." Reuben said this to rescue him from them and take him back to his father. So when Joseph came to his brothers, they stripped him of his robe—the ornate robe he was wearing—and they took him and threw him into the cistern. The cistern was empty; there was no water in it.
> —GENESIS 37:21–24

I love this about Joseph: he was thrown into an empty well, but he chose not to remain empty himself. Terrible things were done to him, yet he did not complain or grow bitter. He kept his eyes on the dream because it was God's promise! His own brothers wanted him dead; but Joseph knew his dream was bigger than their hatred or the well in which they left him.

Here is what you have to remember: God will never leave you where He finds you. No obstacle is bigger than His grace, mercy, and love. Every obstacle *will* change you, but you must decide whether you change for better or worse. You stand between your destiny and your circumstances. You can soar like an eagle with the breath of God under your wings or you can use your circumstances as a crutch to hinder the rest of your life. You can die where you are or dance through the storm, singing praises to God till your joy returns.

So, attention all dreamers: If you plan to reach the next level, if you understand that this is not your destination, if you're determined not to make your current location permanent—then welcome to your well of destiny! You were born to dream and to praise the One who gave you breath.

But you must come to grips with the pit. Face it, Satan wants to take you out. He has been on the attack since the day you were born. He wants you to think you are the only one facing difficulties and hard times. He hopes you will get discouraged, withhold your praise, and walk away from God.

Have you ever wondered why Satan hates it when you praise God and worship with all that is within you? Do you want to know why he works so hard to prevent you from entering into God's courts with praise and thanksgiving? Ezekiel 28 sheds some light on his hatred. Ezekiel tells us that Satan was made of every beautiful and precious stone, and even a living musical instrument. Basically, he was heaven's

Get Your Praise On

worship leader. But in his pride he wanted to be worshipped instead of worshipping the One who created him.

So he was cast out of heaven, and God created us in His own image to have fellowship and relationship with Him. We took Satan's place! God desired intimacy with us. In acknowledging and praising our Creator, we became the worshippers Satan failed to be. No wonder he hates us and does all he can to prevent us from doing what he refused to do.

Worship and praise draw us near to God and bring freedom like nothing else does. Without praise and intimacy with God, we become weary. Our lives become dry as we lose sight of what is important. Then, when we whine and complain and refuse to praise our God, we make life all about us and cry, "Woe is me!" Focused on ourselves and our hardships, we become more and more like the enemy.

Joseph didn't let that happen. He kept pursuing the dream God gave him. Even as a kid there was something special about Joseph and favor rested on His life. His dad, Jacob, gave him a coat of many colors because he loved and favored Joseph. Yet Jacob was a born deceiver (until he wrestled with God and got free). Joseph's brothers hated him because his dream revealed that they would eventually bow down to him. They lied to their father and were willing to kill their sibling. Their family was messed up!

In that atmosphere Joseph's dreams were unwelcome and stirred deadly strife:

> Joseph, a young man of seventeen, was tending the flocks with his brothers, the sons of Bilhah and the sons of Zilpah, his father's wives, and he brought their father a bad report about them. Now Israel loved Joseph more than any of his other sons, because he had been born to him in his old age; and he made an ornate robe for him. When his brothers saw

that their father loved him more than any of them,
they hated him and could not speak a kind word to
him. Joseph had a dream, and when he told it to his
brothers, they hated him all the more. He said to
them, "Listen to this dream I had: We were binding
sheaves of grain out in the field when suddenly my
sheaf rose and stood upright, while your sheaves
gathered around mine and bowed down to it." His
brothers said to him, "Do you intend to reign over
us? Will you actually rule us?" And they hated him
all the more because of his dream and what he had
said. Then he had another dream, and he told it to
his brothers. "Listen," he said, "I had another dream,
and this time the sun and moon and eleven stars
were bowing down to me." When he told his father as
well as his brothers, his father rebuked him and said,
"What is this dream you had? Will your mother and
I and your brothers actually come and bow down to
the ground before you?" His brothers were jealous of
him, but his father kept the matter in mind.

—GENESIS 37:2–11

Joseph was just a teen when God spoke to him through
dreams. He was young and ill-prepared for his brothers'
reaction. Can you relate to his story? Did God give you
any dreams when you were young? Does it feel as though
your dreams have died? Then I'm here to tell you that they
are not dead. It's time to resurrect them—*with your praise.*

Joseph's dreams were fulfilled in the end, but they
were seriously interrupted in his early years. His brothers'
hatred landed Joseph in slavery far from home. His inter-
ruption was long and difficult, but it was not permanent.
Remember this in regard to your dreams. Keep standing
and keep declaring your future, as Joseph did.

Satan cannot stand it when you speak life and declare
your future in God. But God says, He already knows the

plans He has for your life. They are for good and not for harm (Jer. 29:11). All you have to do is walk in obedience and follow the path God has laid out before you. Do it and you will see your dreams fulfilled.

When Joseph was thrown into the pit, he could easily have given up. His whole world came crashing down! His plans for the future had suddenly evaporated. Everything seemed to go horribly wrong. To make matters worse, Joseph's brothers took his coat of many colors, ripped it up, and dipped it in animal blood.

> They took Joseph's coat, butchered a goat, and dipped the coat in the blood. They took the fancy coat back to their father and said, "We found this. Look it over—do you think this is your son's coat?" He recognized it at once. "My son's coat—a wild animal has eaten him. Joseph torn limb from limb!"
> —Genesis 37:31–33, The Message

Joseph was having the worst day of his life. He was attacked, thrown in a dry pit, and left for dead. And his brothers convinced his father that he was dead! All hope seemed lost. I would imagine that Joseph was tempted to throw in the towel.

Have you experienced days, months, or even years like that? I believe most of us have found ourselves in some kind of pit at some point. It's a hard place designed by the enemy to slay your dreams and your praise. But it doesn't have to!

The cistern from which Joseph strained to look up could have finished him off. Everything about it seemed wrong. It was supposed to have water flowing out of it. Instead it was dry. Nothing was flowing in or out. But something changed when Joseph, a crazy, worshipping dreamer, landed in it!

Still, it was a hard place. Your pit is no easier. You may

have given up already. Maybe the pain of your life seems too unbearable and climbing out of the pit seems too hard. But, please don't give up. What you call a pit, God calls a living well of opportunity to bring glory to His name! Lift your hands and praise God for your miracle before it happens, and watch what God does.

He has not deserted you. He knows how to turn around your situation. It is just as Psalm 30:3 says: "You, LORD, brought me up from the realm of the dead; you spared me from going down to the pit." Keep looking to Him. Keep praising Him. Proverbs 17:22 says: "A cheerful heart is good medicine, but a crushed spirit dries up the bones." Praise brings healing oil from heaven to fortify and nourish your spirit.

The pit is a distraction, not your final destination. Realize that you are a worshipper and a dreamer and you are not stopping here. You are going to do what Joseph did: raise the water level by allowing your faith to rise. It will bring you out of the pit into an overflowing wellspring of joy. Then you will say, "He lifted me out of the slimy pit, out of the mud and mire; he set my feet on a rock and gave me a firm place to stand" (Ps. 40:2).

God hears your cries as you lift your voice in praise to Him, the One who gave you life. In the midst of your pit, God will carry you and heal you and set you on a new path to freedom. So praise Him!

> Praise the LORD, my soul, and forget not all his benefits—who forgives all your sins and heals all your diseases, who redeems your life from the pit and crowns you with love and compassion, who satisfies your desires with good things so that your youth is renewed like the eagle's.
>
> —PSALM 103:2–5

Joseph realized that his pit wasn't just a pit; it was the beginning of a great adventure. The Midianites helped to get the adventure underway: "So when the Midianite merchants came by, his brothers pulled Joseph up out of the cistern and sold him for twenty shekels of silver to the Ishmaelites, who took him to Egypt" (Gen. 37:28).

The Midianites represented strife. That's what their name means.[3] Joseph was sold to the Ishmaelites, who took him to Egypt. Their name means, "God will hear"![4] Do you see how God turned Joseph's pit into a beautiful testimony? When he faced terrible strife, God heard his cries and got him out of the pit.

Your pit must become your well. There is a moment when the place you thought would kill you becomes the place where life begins. It is when you are looking up from the pit, straining your neck to see beyond it, that you see Jesus most clearly. Remember: Jesus loves pits! He sat on Jacob's well, the place where the Samaritan woman felt ashamed to go. Jesus waited there to reveal the truth that would set her free. And Jesus went down to the pit of hell for our sakes—to defeat Satan so we could be free for all eternity. That should make the praise rise up in you!

FROM PIT TO OVERFLOWING WELL

How do you turn your pit into a well of living water that overflows to everyone around you? By realizing who is able to rescue you! Reuben rescued Joseph from the threat of death and intended to return him to their father. Reuben's name means "behold a son."[5] Jesus is the Son of God who comes to rescue you out of your pit! I know that when I am in a pit, I need a river of life to flow in. Jesus is the river that never runs dry!

It's time to overflow! Jesus announced the overflow two thousand years ago:

> On the last and greatest day of the festival [feast],
> Jesus stood and said in a loud voice, "Let anyone
> who is thirsty, come to me and drink. Whoever
> believes in me, as the Scripture has said, rivers of
> living water will flow from within him"
>
> —JOHN 7:37–38

Joseph went from the pit, into slavery, into the home of a high official, into prison—and into the palace and his divine purpose. He took a position of authority as governor of the land second only to Pharaoh himself. Joseph's brothers would indeed bow to him and repent and be forgiven. He would save them and his father's entire household. (See Genesis 42–45.)

What I absolutely love about Joseph's story is that, through all the adversity, he continued to believe and refused to become bitter. He walked through great trials and kept praising the King of kings and Lord of lords. Joseph realized it wasn't about him; it was about a far greater cause. Therefore, he never stopped trusting in God or the dream God gave him. He kept the faith, stayed positive, and did not grumble or whine. Despite the storm and the fire, he never wavered or compromised who he was called to be. He stayed the course and continued moving forward. His pit became an overflowing well that saved millions from starvation, spared Egypt from destruction, and kept his own family—the fledgling nation of Israel—alive.

When the enemy throws you in a pit, remember this: "If the Spirit of him who raised Jesus from the dead is living in you, he who raised Christ from the dead will also give life to your mortal bodies because of his Spirit who lives in you" (Rom. 8:11).

God lives in us as believers. *We are the well.* When we get dry, we need only call on His name and He will fill us up again and create in us a living well of refreshing that will also rescue others from dehydration. We must forgive and rescue even our offenders.

Joseph did this despite his brothers' betrayal. His life was a picture of Christ's love for us: even when we turn our backs on Him, He opens His arms wide to us. All we have to do is return to Him and ask forgiveness. In love, He sets us on stable ground and positions us for success.

Just as Joseph was an ambassador to his family, we are called to be ambassadors for Christ in our world. Not long ago, I was headed to Houston to speak at a women's conference. It had been an incredibly hectic week full of school functions and many distractions. I was exhausted. As I boarded my flight, I was hoping to have a row to myself. The week had been so busy that my study time had been limited. I needed to clear my mind during the flight and prepare for the conference.

As the boarding door was closing, it seemed my prayer was answered. I had the entire row to myself! I sighed in relief, thankful to be alone in my row. I was frazzled and really didn't want to talk to anyone. I know—it's crazy! Here I was preparing to preach and tell people about the love of Jesus, right?

Just when I thought the coast was clear, the flight attendant opened the door and a woman who seemed more frazzled than me, ran onto the plane. I scanned the area to see if there was another open seat for her to select. But she kept running toward the back of the plane where I was. Sure enough, she sat down right beside me. I am ashamed to say that I was incredibly disappointed.

Immediately, she started talking to me in a frantic, anxiety-driven tone. I took a deep breath and realized it was going to be a long flight, and there would be no studying. I tried everything in my power to seem dull and uninteresting. I answered each of her incessant questions with a short "Yes," or "No."

Nothing deterred her. She wanted to know everything about me: where I was from, where I was going, and what I had for breakfast. Finally, I closed my binder and looked right at her as she asked, "What do you do for a living? Why are you heading to Houston?"

Her question caught me off guard. After all, I had tried every possible way to avoid her and end the conversation. Now I sat in shame as it hit me: I am an ambassador for Christ! I am a living well of refreshing. What was in me was spilling over to her, and I failed to see it. She was in search of something that I had to give.

How could I miss the opportunity? I put my notes into my briefcase and said, "I'm an evangelist. I'm traveling to Houston to speak at a women's conference."

Immediately her eyes filled up and she said, "I can't believe it. How amazing that God would place me next to you on this flight. I have been in a crisis of faith, not knowing where to turn. And today God answered my prayer. I know there has to be more. Can you help me?"

In that moment I realized that I wasn't just traveling to speak at a women's conference and I wasn't just a traveling evangelist. God lives in me. Just as He has afforded me encounters with Him, He has made me a well of encounter to others who are still searching.

Church, *we are* the well! We are God's encounter to the lost and hurting. As we drink from the well, living water rises in us to the point of overflowing and spills out to everyone with whom we come into contact.

I realized that every pit I'd ever endured had prepared me to be a well of life to this woman. So I spent the rest of that flight ministering the love of Jesus. It was far better conference preparation than anything I could have found in my notes. Even in dry seasons the fountain of living water flows freely when our source is the King!

PRAISE AND A RENEWED MIND

So how do you praise in the midst of the pit? You renew your mind daily. "Do not conform to the pattern of this world, but be transformed by the renewing of your mind. Then you will be able to test and approve what God's will is—his good, pleasing and perfect will" (Rom. 12:2). Renew your mind in God's presence daily, and you will clear out whatever junk the enemy throws at you.

Satan throws all kinds of junk your way: bitterness, anger, unforgiveness, and more. Clean them out daily and pray the prayer David prayed: "Create in me a clean heart, O God, and renew a right, persevering, and steadfast spirit within me" (Ps. 51:10, AMP). David understood the power of praise and of staying in God's presence. The man who faced many trials and seasons of despair and discouragement said this to God: "Do not cast me from your presence or take your Holy Spirit from me. Restore to me the joy of your salvation and grant me a willing spirit, to sustain me" (Ps. 51:11–12).

Satan wants to block your wells by perverting your worship. He wants you to worship your own pleasures instead of your Creator. He knows that if you enter into praise and thanksgiving, your joy will return. This is exactly what the Samaritan woman learned. Her people worshiped every god except the one true God! But then she found her Messiah, and her years of despair turned to joy.

God wants you all to Himself. He wants a loving, intimate relationship with you. That is the true worship and true relationship Jesus offered to the Samaritan woman. It was the relationship with her Father—the relationship every human being craves.

It's time to put the devil back under our feet where he belongs. I already mentioned how he hates us. He wants us not to praise and worship God because that is what he was created to do. But here is the most amazing thing: Revelation 21 says that the streets of heaven are made of pure gold and the foundation of its wall is made with precious stones. We will tread upon every precious stone that Satan refused to worship God with! We become the choir of worshippers that sing praises to the King! We took Satan's place. We took his job.

So, come on and get your praise on!

A Moment at the Well

Praise today! Praise God for where you are and where you are going! Realize that you have not yet arrived. This adventure is just beginning. Declare today that no matter what, there will be praise on your lips. Declare: "I will bless the LORD at all times; His praise will continually be in my mouth" (Ps. 34:1, MEV). Jesus will become life in the midst of your chaos *if* you will praise Him in it. For even the storm obeys His commands. He is worthy of your praise. As you praise Him right now, I challenge you—*stay* in His presence and feel the rain from heaven as it falls upon you and refreshes you. Get filled to the point of overflowing—and overflow!

Chapter 9

BE BRAVE

Be brave. Be strong. Don't give up.
Expect GOD to get here soon.
—PSALM 31:24, THE MESSAGE

W HEN YOU WAKE up and look in the mirror, do you see a mighty warrior dressed for battle? Do you feel brave? What is *brave* anyway? That is what this chapter is about: redefining our ideas about being brave and proving that we *can be* brave!

There are so many words I could use to describe the seasons and journey of my life. One word that I have never used in this regard is the word *brave*. Often I describe my Christian walk as constant, steady, passionate, and even desperate—but not brave. I had to take a closer look at that. Now it's time for us to look at it together and find out what bravery really is.

When you face physical or spiritual dehydration, you find strength and courage you never thought you had. My hope is that you will see that and realize that you have been much braver than you think. The truth is that you are a mighty warrior for God and He has equipped you for battle. So step up! Take heart. God is about to use you! You are a child of the King—the King who has planned your every breath and has walked you through every struggle and triumph!

It might surprise you to hear this, but bravery is not necessarily the absence of fear. It is the realization that fear cannot rule you because you reside in the presence

of God. I am extremely grateful and blessed to live in a
land of freedom. I am also very grateful for our nation's
first responders who face grave dangers and even violence
on a daily basis, just to keep us safe. The freedom we possess comes with a price. Many have lost their lives for us.
Our family honors those who fight and risk it all for our
freedom. Those men and women are brave indeed. They
are heroes in my eyes!

While such sacrifices are obvious examples of bravery, I
have learned that bravery comes in other forms. It is not
only running into a burning building or standing on a
foreign battlefield fighting the enemy. Sometimes bravery
means standing up for truth and for what is right and just
and holy. Sometimes it is the ability to look adversity and
even tragedy in the eye and say, "I'm not quitting—period!"

Satan uses many tactics to try and cripple us, but one of
his greatest tools is fear. He wants to keep us in bondage
to fear in order to prevent us from reaching the purpose
and plans God has laid out before us.

Have you sensed his attempts? Fear dehydrates your
spirit when it drives you into isolation. When you hide,
you stop seeking the life-giving water you so desperately
need. Your fear not only dehydrates you; it also affects
your family. They need a brave and courageous warrior
who will risk it all to protect and preserve the spiritual
wells in your home.

Whether it's the fear of failure, fear of your past, fear of
man, or just fear of the unknown, God wants you to know
that you don't have to fear anything or anyone if you are
with Him. Walking with God brings the ultimate security,
confidence, and boldness. This is particularly true when
you thoroughly grasp his power, authority, and might.

God is the Almighty One. None can compare with Him.
Walk with God and you will be brave. Let the Holy Spirit

encourage you with these words: "I'm sure now I'll see God's goodness in the exuberant earth. Stay with GOD! Take heart. Don't quit. I'll say it again: Stay with GOD" (Ps. 27:13–14, THE MESSAGE).

Freedom comes when you catch hold of the fact that God is stronger and more powerful than anything or anyone that could ever come against you. Scripture says it plainly: "The one who is in you is greater than the one who is in the world" (1 John 4:4). Start believing it! It's real! The enemy knows how real it is, so his goal is to keep you from buying in. Why? Because the minute you believe, you will be unstoppable!

How do I know? I know by experience. I am living it! For most of my early life, fear was my constant companion. At every crossroads and from around every corner, fear taunted me. I shared with you how shy I was in my youth. It was *debilitating*. That fear and shyness followed me into my adult life so that, in the early years of marriage and parenthood I learned to hide and mask my fear.

But it was always there. I was afraid of failure, so I would avoid trying new things or reaching beyond my comfort zone. I was afraid of crowds because I feared looking stupid or being embarrassed. I hid it well, but it caused great anxiety for me.

I'll never forget when Pat and I were youth pastors. We planned a retreat for our youth group and Pat decided that we needed a session just for the girls. I completely agreed. Pat had scheduled Roosevelt Hunter to speak to our students. I assumed that we would find a powerful female speaker who would speak life, purity, and purpose into the lives of the girls.

A couple of weeks passed without any further discussion, so I asked Pat whether he had thought about a speaker for the girls' session. He smiled and said, "Yes, I have already scheduled it." He handed me the retreat flyer, which he had so conveniently printed off ahead of time. I remember wondering why he had not consulted me or asked my opinion beforehand. As I read through the flyer, it became clear why he had kept it from me: *I was the speaker.*

My heart pounded and immediately, I felt nauseated. I quickly pointed out that there had been a misprint and he needed to correct it before he distributed the flyers. He said, "There was no mistake, Karen. I believe in you. God has called you and given you a voice and a word for the girls of this generation."

I had never spoken publicly. I saw myself as more of a one-on-one person. Honestly, I simply did not feel qualified. With all my fear and insecurities, what would I have to impart to these girls? I tried to back out of the assignment, but it was no use. It had been announced and that was that.

I wish I could say that I rose to the challenge and embraced the new adventure, but I was scared to death. I am a stubborn person, so I may or may not have carried a grudge against Pat during the two weeks leading up to the retreat. I am so blessed to have a husband who saw God's call on my life despite my fear and insecurities. He saw in me those things that I could not yet see. He believed in me when I didn't believe in myself.

As the retreat approached, I was sick to my stomach, I broke out in hives, and I was a nervous wreck—a mess! I look back and laugh at that girl now since I hardly recognize her. I'm sure my family sometimes wishes that I wasn't as bold and outspoken as I am now. But something happened during that retreat: I found my strength, my courage, and my voice. I found them because of the One who revealed them to me, my Father God, who has walked with me since I was thirteen years old—the One who said

He would never leave nor forsake me. He awakened me to my purpose and destiny. As a result, I stopped seeing myself as that little, shy, insecure, weak, thirteen-year-old girl. Instead I saw a bold, courageous, and empowered woman who was a victorious overcomer.

The enemy didn't win; God won! With help from my husband and God, I pushed past the trap that the enemy had set for me. He discovered that he could not hold me there any longer. I had not only survived, but God had led me to victory, which was precisely the message a generation of girls needed to hear. Like me, they were not weak, insecure little girls. They were mighty warriors for God!

I discovered that week that if all I am living for is me, then I will always walk in fear; but when I live for God's purposes, *nothing* can hold me back. "Have I not commanded you? Be strong and courageous. Do not be afraid; do not be discouraged, for the LORD your God will be with you wherever you go" (Josh. 1:9).

CONFRONT THE PHANTOM OF YOUR OPERA

All of us have contended with our share of messes. In the opera called life, phantoms can linger in the shadows, taunting and intimidating us. But I say, "Stop!" Stop chasing the ghosts of past failures and the family demons that have haunted you for years. Step forward with courage into the story God is writing for your life. It is a story of victory, destiny, and legacy for you and your family.

What is keeping you from approaching the well of refreshing and freedom from fear? Don't be ashamed to face it. I have seen fear in the eyes of people all across this nation. Not only that, but have I experienced it! It shows up in the eyes of a hurting child, a wounded wife, a lonely man who has lost everything. Fear can debilitate you. I know this firsthand! But it doesn't have to rule your life. If you will fix your eyes on things that are eternal, you can push past your fears.

Fear can mute the voice of God and amplify the snarl of the enemy. It keeps you backed into a corner and hidden in the looming shadows of night. God is calling you into the light to shine brightly and guide others to Him. You are called to arise and stand firm! When others quit, you don't have a right to quit! The enemy wants to convince you that the fight is too hard or too dangerous. He's hoping you will back down. He used this tactic on Job, and Job said, "I try to make the best of it, try to brave it out, but you're too much for me, relentless, like a lion on the prowl" (Job 10:16, THE MESSAGE).

The enemy attacks and pursues you in your weakness. He is bold and brazen and knows just when to shove you into a corner. He knows your insecurities and how to cripple your emotions. But he is a liar! The Bible says so in John 8:44. There is no truth in him—*none*. He is a terrorist whose goal is to immobilize you with fear! But God goes before you and watches behind you. "So we say with confidence, 'The Lord is my helper; I will not be afraid. What can mere mortals do to me?'" (Heb. 13:6).

Can I tell you something? *You are still here.* That means you have survived battles, pushed through pain, and clung to the cross for hope. That is what I call brave! Keep at it and see what happens:

> You'll take delight in God, the Mighty One, and look to him joyfully, boldly. You'll pray to him and he'll listen; he'll help you do what you've promised. You'll decide what you want and it will happen; your life will be bathed in light. To those who feel low you'll say, "Chin up! Be brave!" and God will save them.
> —JOB 22:26–29, THE MESSAGE

Bravery comes in many shapes and sizes. Some extraordinary people in my life are very brave. I have watched them take down all kinds of phantoms. Chief among them is my husband. He is the bravest man I know. I am amazed at the stand he takes for integrity and truth. He is brave in all that he does out of love for our family. He is brave in his pursuit of God in a culture that waters down the truth of the gospel.

My daughter Abby is brave beyond comprehension. She has overcome so much in her life and continues to praise God for all that He has done for her. Her love and passion for life amaze me. My son Nate is also very brave and continues to overcome. He is a walking miracle and an example of God's power to defeat the enemy's plans. Even as Nate dealt with daily pain and spinal discomfort caused by Scheuermann's kyphosis,[1] he continually pressed through, never complaining or letting it affect what he had to do each and every day. Doctors were stunned by his ability to function so well despite his pain. Until his physical issue progressed to the point of affecting his posture, most people didn't know Nate was dealing with physical challenges.

I shared in Chapter 6 about how Nate had to give up his dream of playing college football, due to spinal disease and injury. That event could have sucked the life out of him, but it did not. It propelled him into his destiny! What the enemy wanted to use to kill him instead brought him to a new level of understanding God's purpose and power in his life.

After Nate gave up football and wholeheartedly pursued God's call on his life, his back pain let up a bit. The relief would be short-lived. The fact that he was not taking the constant hits to his spine made a huge difference, but the battle was not over. Scheuermann's kyphosis can cause the spine to bend forward over time, potentially with crippling effects. We had hoped that it would not progress and Nate would be able to continue without surgery. This did not prove to be the case. His spinal curvature did progress. It became increasingly painful and significantly affected his daily life.

We did our research to find the best doctor and facility and were referred to a doctor in Houston—the top doctor in his field for this particular condition. We headed to Houston to meet with him and find out what could be done for Nate. After a series of exams, tests, and x-rays, we were told that surgery was the only possible way to correct the condition.

Surgery is always a last resort; it is invasive and can lead to complications. This particular procedure is complex. It was not exactly the solution we wanted to hear. We talked it over as a family and prayed and prayed and prayed. Finally Nate said he wanted to have the surgery. He was tired of having to deal with the issue and wanted to move on with his life. He and Adrienne were expecting their first child and he wanted nothing to prevent him from holding his baby and playing and participating in the child's life. Left unchecked, Nate's spinal condition would eventually hinder all of that. So his mind was made up; he would have the surgery.

I have to admit that during the months leading up to the surgery, I struggled with fear and anxiety over the intensity of what Nate was facing. I did not feel very brave and I could not imagine what he was feeling. Part of me wanted him to cancel the procedure, but the other part didn't want to stand in the way of his freedom from pain. No parent wants to see his or her child in pain; but no parent wants a child to undergo a potentially life-altering procedure, either. Nevertheless, I knew Nate's decision was based on his desire for a better quality of life; I respected his decision and supported him in it.

As the date of the surgery approached, we went to Houston and settled into our hotel rooms. The night before the procedure, we went out to eat and had a wonderful time of prayer, laughter, and more prayer. Someone at the table popped the question: "Do you still want to do this?"

Nate's answer was definite: "Yes!" He and Adrienne were both very brave.

After dinner we returned to our rooms in hopes of getting some rest. We knew the coming days would be long and difficult, and Nate would remain in the hospital for at least a week. We wanted to be ready.

The morning of surgery followed a long, sleepless night. There was little conversation during the walk to the hospital, but there was a lot of intercession. Not only were we praying that day, but hundreds of people across the nation were lifting our son and family in prayer. I am still overwhelmed at the army of prayer warriors that joined in the fight, not only that day but through the weeks and even months that followed.

As the saying goes, "you just gotta love" the brutal honesty of physicians in the moments before they wheel you into surgery. Nate's doctor looked at us and wanted to make sure we fully understood the risks. (I can assure you I had done more research than I should have and was fully aware of *every* risk involved.) The doctor looked at us and proceeded to say that Nate could lose his life during surgery or bleed out and need a blood transfusion or be paralyzed or crippled. Furthermore, the surgery might not succeed at all.

Although I already knew all that, hearing the doctor say it aloud was like having a bomb drop in the room. I think

Pat considered snatching Nate out of the bed and saying, "Forget it!" I would have gladly helped him do it.

However, one of the most memorable moments came when the hospital chaplain came to pray with both patient and family. Keep in mind that when the chaplain entered the room, he was in no way prepared to face four Spirit-filled preachers. But he walked in with a prepared speech and his soft-spoken, intentionally soothing voice and said, "Let's take hands and pray."

That is as far as the chaplain got with his speech, because in that moment, power, authority, and faith rose up in Pat! Faith and a holy anger toward the enemy rose up in all of us. There would be no preplanned cozy little rehearsed prayers prayed over our son that day. Nor would there be any prayers from someone who knew neither our son nor the call on his life.

Pat looked over at the chaplain and with authority in his voice, declared, "I got this! Thank you, but I will lead this prayer over my son today!"

Pat prayed the prayer of faith *powerfully*. He prayed that God's presence would fill that operating room and that God would guide the surgeon's hands. He prayed that there would be no complications and no transfusion. He prayed for the surgery to be a complete success and for Nate to make a full recovery, in Jesus's name.

We called down heaven in that tiny, little room. Needless to say, the chaplain could not wait to get away from us crazy people. We did not see him again for the duration of Nate's hospitalization. There is a time for sweet prayers and there is a time for warring prayers. We were ready for war. The enemy would be defeated. The message of Psalm 46:1 became so real to us: "God is our refuge and strength, an ever present help in trouble."

As they wheeled Nate into surgery, Pat headed to a

secluded area to pray. Adrienne went to another area to pray, notify family members, and provide updates. I found somewhere to get alone with God. There was a six-to seven-hour wait ahead and I needed to find my peace in Him. I remember crying out to God to be with my boy throughout the surgery and not leave him. I found out later that Pat and Adrienne both prayed the same thing. How awesome it was that we were all in different places but the God of the universe met each of us where we were. And still, He remained by Nate's side. We serve a mighty God!

When I cried out God spoke to me once again, as He has done throughout my life. He reminded me of when Nate was two years old and safe in his car seat behind me as I drove. Whenever we were in the car, we gave each other air hugs and kisses so he would feel like he was with me. Once, when we were out running errands, I took advantage of a quiet moment to pray. You moms know how hard it is to find quiet time when caring for a toddler

I had just prayed that God would make Himself known to Nate. I asked that, even at his early age, Nate would know how much God loved him. Then all of a sudden Nate gave a great big air hug and kiss from the back seat. I asked him, "What are you doing, sweetheart?"

He replied, "Jesus just gave me a big hug and kiss!"

Tears flowed down my cheeks as I realized that Jesus had answered my prayer! Nate really did get a hug and kiss from Jesus and knew, at his young age, how much God loved him.

Now, with a grown-up Nate in surgery, God reminded me of that moment. He did it to show me that I was not in control, but He was. He was with Nate just as He had been in the back seat of our car many years ago. Nate was in the safest place he could be—in the arms of Jesus!

The same God who met me in the school courtyard when I was thirteen met me once again. The same God who met my husband in the basement of his home when he was sixteen—saving him and transforming him—was with us that day. The same God who met me in my deep despair as I sat parked in my garage, and opened my eyes to see my beautiful daughter from a distant land, was there with us that day!

Bravery is choosing to open your eyes and see what God wants you to see in the midst of the chaos all around you. As my eyes opened, peace flooded the room and the warmth of God's presence was all that was needed. We spent the next several hours waiting and praying and speaking life to one another as people came by to show their support and stand with us. Every update we received was good news.

After five hours in surgery, the doctor came out and shared his report. He said that Nate had done wonderfully, much better than expected. There had been no complications and he did not lose nearly as much blood as they feared he might. No transfusion would be needed and Nate was expected to make a full recovery. Praise God!

The good news may have surprised the doctors, but not us. God had already given each of us a sense of peace and confidence that the outcome would be great. During the next few days in the hospital, Nate faced many obstacles, however. He found it difficult to stand, sit, and walk; but he pushed past every obstacle with determination and courage. He insisted on exceeding the minimum required physical therapy. Doing so meant he had to fight to overcome the pain, stiffness, and all the drugs he had to take. My boy became an even more powerful man in my eyes that week.

The road to recovery was not easy. One night Nate was in excruciating pain, even while on morphine, Oxycontin, and Lortab. He said it felt like a chainsaw was cutting through his back. Pat and I had gone to our room to get a few hours of sleep. Our precious daughter-in-love, Adrienne, would not leave Nate's side and was sleeping in a chair by his bed. Nate said the pain was so intense and unbearable that he did not know whether he would make it through the night.

Then Nate cried out to God, expressing how much he needed God's presence and help to get through this. In that moment, he opened his eyes and saw at the foot of his bed a beautiful, glowing being with His arms outstretched toward him. He knew it was Jesus, and he was not afraid.

Jesus said to him, "I'm right here with you, Nate. You're not alone and I won't leave you."

Nate said the pain was still there, yet he was able to close his eyes and fall asleep in peace. *We serve a mighty God* who is also *a loving Father*! He will never leave us nor forsake us (Heb. 13:5).

Nate said that although his surgery is the most painful thing he has ever gone through, and despite the fact that his recovery has been long and difficult, it was worth it, for more than just the physical reasons. It was worth it because any doubts or second thoughts Nate might have had about who God is disappeared in that single moment in his hospital room. How could he ever doubt or turn his back on the One who showed up that night? Nate can never, ever walk away. God is all he needs, and he will spend the rest of his life showing people the only Way to find Him. Nate's testimony has already ministered life and hope to so many people!

To add to our beautiful family testimony, Nate and Adrienne blessed us with our first grandson on December 21, 2014. Nate was able to pick up his son, hold him, and carry him with no pain or limitations. Praise God! Nate, Adrienne, and Jackson will change the world for God.

Even as you rejoice in our testimony, you may be thinking that you have walked through too many ordeals or experienced too much pain to ever have a testimony of your own. You feel as though the issues you face have drained your life away. You have become dry, weary, and dehydrated, and cannot seem to find the well of refreshing.

I want you to know that walking through trials and fires and taking hits on the battlefield don't make you weak or wounded. They make you brave! The enemy's arrows have grazed you. You carry the scars of a warrior who has outlasted the battle. You are called to go and rescue others and lead them to the same freedom you gain. Because you have survived, you are prepared to fight and lead them to the One who can save, heal, and set them free.

I am so dismayed at the distorted view of bravery that is embraced across the nation right now. Some have declared that *bravery* means publicly declaring a perverse lifestyle and calling it *normal*. Others think it is brave for evil people to blow up themselves and others in the name of a false religion. Causing mayhem and bloodshed in the marketplace is not brave. The fact that anyone would think so proves how desperately we need to understand what true bravery is! Culture has tried to redefine it. The distortion eats away at truth like dripping water eats away at stone. The attack is often subtle, but it is effective.

We must stand strong! The brave declare that God is the Lord of all! Bravery means saying that He has called us to live lives of purpose, passion, and destiny. He has called us to overcome and conquer and set the captives free! When God becomes the Lord of our hearts, we see the world through His eyes and not the eyes of fear.

WHAT BRAVERY IS

Remember that bravery comes in many forms. Here are some everyday examples:

- Bravery is a beautiful young lady with Down syndrome showing up at prom and hoping someone will dance with her because she understands that she is fearfully and wonderfully made (Ps. 139:14).

- Bravery is a single mom juggling two jobs to make ends meet and still finding time to read bedtime stories to her babies because she understands that they are what really matters.

- Bravery is a widow who delays going to bed until the last possible moment then slides her foot over to the cold, empty side of her bed where her husband had lain beside her for fifty years—still knowing that God will never forsake her.

- Bravery is a missionary who travels for days to a remote village armed only with a message of hope and freedom, knowing God loves every soul.

- Bravery is smiling through fear and anguish as a needle pierces a worn-out vein to stop the cancer that is destroying your child's body, because you know that your child's strength depends on seeing your own faith arise.

- Bravery is worshipping through the storm when your heart is broken, knowing that God is all you need.

- Bravery is realizing that your bank account is empty days before payday, but knowing that God shall supply all your needs according to His riches and glory by Christ Jesus (Phil. 4:19).

- Bravery is clinging to one last hope that your spouse will someday find the way back home.

- Bravery is standing up alone for biblical truth while the culture declares that you are out of touch.

- Bravery is calling and encouraging your child who is in a distant land defending freedom, while you are weeping on the inside, realizing it was for freedom that we have been set free.

- Bravery is standing firm on your convictions when you know it will cost you your friends.

- Bravery is declaring that you will not bow to what did not die for you.

- Bravery is believing without seeing, and saying, "I will not quit, back down, or abandon the truth."

- Bravery is declaring that Jesus is Lord as you lose your life for the gospel's sake.

Bravery—your bravery—has many faces. Quit letting the enemy back you into a corner. Don't let him steal your ability to stand. Many fears may tempt you, but you need only one: the holy fear of God! It is a fear that says, "I'm in awe of Your greatness, God, and I give myself wholly to You."

Are you living under constant attack from the enemy? Do you want to know why? It is because the enemy sees in your eyes the reflection of the holy, just, and fearsome God! You are the apple of God's eye (Ps. 17:8, NKJV). The enemy has to see you through that lens. He recognizes the anger of God that arises when Satan attacks you, His child. Satan sees that you are fearfully and wonderfully made. He knows that God is a fiercely protective Father. He knows that God has invested a great deal in you and will never leave nor forsake you—*ever.*

Cry out to God! Not man, not positions, not culture, but God!

> Take my side, God—I'm getting kicked around, stomped on every day. Not a day goes by but somebody beats me up; they make it their duty to beat me up. When I get really afraid I come to you in trust. I'm proud to praise God; fearless now, I trust in God. What can mere mortals do?
> —PSALM 56:1–4, THE MESSAGE

Our bravery comes from knowing and understanding that our strength comes from God alone. That is *enough.* It is all we need.

I hope you are getting this. You are brave when you walk past your doubters, your mockers, and those who have given up on you. In your bravery, you bring power down from Jesus! Your bravery stops Him in His tracks. He does not let it go unnoticed! He takes you by the hand and lifts you out of your pit. He sets your feet on stable ground and puts you back on track to a life of freedom from the very things the enemy used in hopes of killing you. God is watching. He is looking for the brave ones. He calls you out beyond where you have been.

When you realize that God's arms are open and He wants to heal, restore, and rescue you, bravery becomes second nature. As your awe of Him increases, your fear of man is diminished. When your eyes are fixed on God, everything else shrinks in the light of His power.

BEAUTIFUL SCARS

We started this journey together talking about the encounter between Jesus and the woman at the well. (See John 4.) She didn't deserve Jesus's kindness or generosity, but God saw past her reputation and shame. He *wanted* to give her new life. He wants to do the same for you and me. He has the power to completely set us free *with one encounter,* one drink from the well.

It is so empowering when you awaken to the reality that God loves you, you're not alone, and you can be brave and overcome every obstacle. That is what happened to the Samaritan woman. At the well she learned to live again. Suddenly, she discovered her purpose in life. She encountered a Savior who loved her despite her history, and beyond it. Then He introduced her His-story!

God wants us to experience the joy of freedom. It is a freedom that transforms. The Samaritan woman's encounter with Jesus was so transformational that she and her entire city were changed! Her story brought life to others.

Our stories can bring life to others, too! God has called us to get up and live a life worth living. The woman at the well didn't waste her moment. She became an evangelist. She was so overwhelmed with the love of God that she ran right back to those who had rejected her and shared the God who would never reject them.

It is amazing to me that God would use such a broken, bruised, and rejected woman to tell a city about Jesus. It shows that God can use you no matter what you have been through, no matter what your past holds. The woman at the well was deeply scarred by rejection and pain, but her scars became her testimony.

We all have scars whether they are physical, mental, or emotional. But can I tell you something? Your scars are proof that you have survived. Never be ashamed of them. A scar means the hurt is over and the wound is closed. God healed you and you are still here. You're no longer a victim of your past. Instead, you are a victor and a survivor! Quit looking back at the "what ifs," the "could've beens," and the "should've beens." Just realize that you survived! Stop complaining and start rejoicing that you have overcome.

What you survive should make you stronger, just like the caterpillar-turned-butterfly. Without the struggle your strength could never take flight. Because the Samaritan woman had been such a mess, people wanted to see the One who could heal their messes! What you walk through is a good indication of whom you are called to reach. Jesus knew that the woman at the well would get past herself and see the masses. He knows you will, too.

God knows exactly where you are and is preparing some time alone with you. He wants to tell you about the huge plan He has for your life. Sometimes you have to get to a place of brokenness before you can have a transforming encounter with Him. Then, at the well of refreshing, you find our purpose: to go into all the world, tell them about Jesus, train them in all His ways, and let them know that He will be with them until the very end! (See Matthew 28:16–20.)

When the city folks saw the Samaritan woman running back from the well without her water pot, they probably thought she was crazy. "What in the world is the town pariah about to say?" they wondered.

Their opinions no longer intimidated her. She did not care about her reputation anymore. She was so overwhelmed by the love encounter she'd just had with Jesus that she bravely threw away her fears. That is what His love does! "There is no fear in love. But perfect love drives out fear" (1 John 4:18).

The Samaritan woman's changed demeanor made people come and listen to what she had to say. When people see your transformation, they will be curious. When they see you go from being bent over, dehydrated, and weary to vibrant and full of life, they will want to hear about what has happened to you. God will be so strong in you that they will do a double take. Your transformation will make them realize that they are just as lost as you used to be.

Know what your role is: you're not in sales; you're in advertising. Your life screams, "Freedom!"

Are you getting this? Bravery takes you past who you used to be, so others can see who changed you. You will be known by your fruit, and it will be good fruit. The goodness of God in you will lead others to repentance. (See Matthew 7:16; Romans 2:4.)

When we become willing to lay down the clay pot by the well, God can fill it with whatever is missing in our lives. The clay pot represents an empty vessel. The Samaritan woman laid down the old vessel behind which she had hidden herself for years. It had been her security blanket—until she found her security in a loving Savior!

God puts treasures in jars of clay (2 Cor. 4:7). Even though the woman at the well had been such a mess, Jesus recognized the treasure and orchestrated an encounter that would spark a fire and transform a city. Will you be that encounter for your life, the lives of your loved ones, and the life of your city?

HE MADE ME BRAVE

A certain song has touched me deeply. It is called "You Make Me Brave."[2] It talks about how God's love makes us brave and calls away from the shoreline and into deeper waters. He longs for us to touch heaven and the hem of His garment, knowing that all things are possible in Him, not just the easy, comfortable things. That is bravery! It means understanding that Satan was meant to be under our feet and we have authority in God to defeat him. Bravery means we finally understand that when the Book ends, God wins—and because He lives in us, *we win*.

Despite the fact that my life began in shyness, fear, and feelings of worthlessness, I met a man at a well named Jesus! That amazing and loving Man invaded my life, set me free, and sent me on a journey and great adventure. No matter how dry and weary life is at times, I know where the well is and I choose to never stop drinking from it. It is the well of living water that my Savior gives me.

In my freedom, I realized that I could not remain the same. I had to tell everyone about the freedom I found in Him. When His love and freedom invade your life, it is impossible to keep it to yourself. You have to share it with everyone you meet. You cannot walk away from the dehydrated masses. You realize that God wants to invade our world—and He wants to use you and me to do it. He wants our lives to impact others so they can be free.

It is time to run to the lost and tell them about the Man at the well. Today, I stand on stages around the world proclaiming the hope, truth, and freedom that Jesus brings. If God can use me, He can use anyone. It took many years for me to realize that the courtyard bench or "well" encounters I had with Jesus were never really about me. He invited me to have them so others could experience the courtyard-bench Savior for themselves.

I have realized that success in life is not determined by popularity, positions, titles, or bank accounts. Success in life is determined by the impact we leave on those who are left behind when we are gone. Did we make them thirsty for God? Did we lead them to the well so they could have their own encounters with Jesus? Did we point them toward the well that would sustain them for a lifetime and for eternity?

We *must* go and tell the world. If we don't, who will?

A MOMENT AT THE WELL

Declare today that you will meet Jesus at the well of your life and you will become undone and untangled from the enemy's snares. If you do not know Jesus, but you want to meet Him, become new, and commit your life to the only life-giver, then this is your moment. Lift your voice to heaven and accept the free gift of salvation from God the Father. Simply accept the love and forgiveness He is offering you right now. He loves you and meets you where you are. Pray according to Romans 10:9, which says: "If you declare with your mouth, 'Jesus is LORD,' and believe in your heart that God raised him from the dead, you will be saved." Declare that you will not grow weary but will continually return to the well of truth and freedom. Declare that you will keep a shovel in your hand so you can continually clear the well and keep it flowing freely. Declare that God is not done with you or your family; tell Him that you will protect His presence and leave a legacy.

Let hope arise today and be *brave*. God is standing right in front of you, right now. His arms are outstretched, ready to embrace you. The God of the universe is waiting to walk this journey with you. Embrace it!

Life is a great adventure with God, and He wants us to embrace the journey!

NOTES

CHAPTER 1
CONVERSATIONS WITH THE KING

1. Biblestudy.org, "Meaning of Numbers in the Bible: The Number 5," http://www.biblestudy.org/bibleref/meaning-of-numbers-in-bible/5.html (accessed March 12, 2015).
2. Biblestudy.org, "Meaning of Numbers in the Bible: The Number 6," http://www.biblestudy.org/bibleref/meaning-of-numbers-in-bible/6.html (accessed March 12, 2015).
3. Biblestudy.org, "Meaning of Numbers in the Bible: The Number 7," http://www.biblestudy.org/bibleref/meaning-of-numbers-in-bible/7.html (accessed March 12, 2015).
4. Google.com, "Metamorphosis," https://www.google.com/search?client=safari&rls=en&q=definition+of+Metamorphosis&ie=UTF-8&oe=UTF-8&expnd=1&brd=1421794720849000 (accessed March 12, 2015).
5. Ibid.
6. YourDictionary.com, s.v. "chrysalis," http://www.yourdictionary.com/chrysalis (accessed March 12, 2015).
7. Jews hated Samaritans because they believed the Samaritans had turned away from the religion of their fathers. To the Jews, Samaritans were therefore seen as traitors.

CHAPTER 2
I AM UNDONE!

1. Biblesoft's *New Exhaustive Strong's Numbers and Concordance With Expanded Greek-Hebrew Dictionary*, Biblesoft Inc. and International Bible Translators Inc., 2006, s.v. "damah," (OT 1820).

CHAPTER 3

FAMINE

1. Andy Park, "Let It Rain," Mercy/Vineyard Publishing, 1996.
2. BibleTools.org,"Bible Verses About Amos the Prophet," http://www.Bibletools.org/index.cfm/fuseaction/Topical .show/RTD/cgg/ID/1131/Amos-Prophet.htm (accessed March 14, 2015).
3. GotQuestions.org, "Book of Amos," http://www .gotquestions.org/Book-of-Amos.html#ixzz3PcJ02PnX (accessed March 9, 2015).
4. Insight for Living Ministries, "Amos," http://www.insight .org/resources/bible/amos.html (accessed March 9, 2015).
5. Dictionary.com, s.v. "famine," http://dictionary.reference .com/browse/famine (accessed: March 9, 2015).
6. Oxfam International, "Famine in Somalia: Causes and Solutions," http://www.oxfam.org/en/somalia/famine -somalia-causes-and-solutions (accessed March 9, 2015).
7. Urban Dictionary, http://www.urbandictionary.com/define .php?term=Thirsty, s.v. "thirsty" (accessed March 14, 2015).
8. National Center for HIV/AIDS, Viral Hepatitis, STD, and TB Prevention, Centers for Disease Control, "HIV and Other STD Prevention and United States Students," http://www .cdc.gov/healthyyouth/yrbs/pdf/us_hiv_combo.pdf (accessed March 14, 2015).
9. ChurchLeaders.com,"7 Startling Facts: An Up Close Look at Church Attendance in America," http://www.churchleaders .com/pastors/pastor-articles/139575-7-startling-facts-an-up -close-look-at-church-attendance-in-america.html (accessed March 14, 2015).
10. Heather Clark, "Megachurch Leader Claims 'Divine Wind' Moved Him to Fully Accept Members Practicing Homosex- uality," Christian News Network, January 30, 2015, http:// christiannews.net/2015/01/30/megachurch-leader-claims -divine-wind-moved-him-to-fully-accept-members -practicing-homosexuality/ (accessed March 9, 2015).
11. Biblegateway.com, "Romans 7:5," footnote a, https://www .biblegateway.com/passage/?search=rom+7%3A5&version =NIV (accessed June 29, 2015).
12. Taz Loomans, "Earth Day Network Plants 350,000 Trees in Uganda, Aims to Plant 10 Million Trees in 5 Years," Inhab- itat, December 18, 2012, http://inhabitat.com/earth-day

-network-plants-350000-trees-in-uganda-aims-to-plant-10
-million-trees-in-5-years/ (accessed March 9, 2015).

CHAPTER 4
REDIG THE ANCIENT WELLS

1. Pat Schatzline, *I Am Remnant: Discover the Power to Stand for Truth in a Changing Culture* (Lake Mary, FL: Charisma Media, 2014), xx.
2. Leonard Ravenhill, "Revival Series, Lecture 1," ravenhill .org, http://www.ravenhill.org/revival1.htm (accessed March 9, 2015).
3. Leonard Ravenhill, "Weeping Between the Porch and the Altar—Part I," ravenhill.org, http://www.ravenhill.org /weeping1.htm (accessed March 9, 2015).
4. Wayne Blank, "Esek, Sitnah, Rehoboth," Daily Study Bible, http://www.keyway.ca/htm2006/20060814.htm (accessed March 10, 2015).
5. The Online Bible Thayer's Greek Lexicon and Brown Driver & Briggs' Hebrew Lexicon (Ontario: Woodside Bible Fellowship, 1993), s.v. "Sitnah" (OT 7856).
6. Father's House Ministries, "Prelude to a Revival," http:// www.fathershouseministries.org/images/Prelude_to_a _Revival,_20120923.pdf (accessed March 15, 2015).

CHAPTER 5
THE POWER OF THE AFTERMATH

1. Dictionary.com, s.v. "aftermath," http://dictionary.reference .com/browse/aftermath (accessed: March 10, 2015).
2. Ibid.

CHAPTER 6
IT AIN'T OVER

1. Bethany Hamilton, *Soul Surfer* (New York: Simon & Schuster, 2004), 87.
2. SheKnows.com, s.v. "Abigail," http://www.sheknows.com /baby-names/name/abigail (accessed March 16, 2015).
3. Goodreads.com, "Marianne Williamson Quotes," http:// www.goodreads.com/author/quotes/17297.Marianne _Williamson (accessed March 10, 2015).
4. Saying Quotes, "C. S. Lewis," https://sites.google.com/site /sayingquotes/cs-lewis (accessed March 10, 2015).

CHAPTER 7
HOPE FLOATS

1. *Thayer's Greek Lexicon* (Electronic Database), Biblesoft Inc., 2003, s.v. "zoe" (NT 2222).
2. Ibid., s.v. "perissos" (NT 4053).
3. TheFreeDictionary.com, s.v. "despair," http://www.thefree dictionary.com/despair (accessed March 11, 2015).
4. Wordnik.com, s.v. "hope,"https://www.wordnik.com/words /hope (accessed March 17, 2015).

CHAPTER 8
GET YOUR PRAISE ON

1. It happened in Acts 2.
2. Gotquestions.org, "What Is the Meaning of the Greek Word *Dunamis* in the Bible?," http://www.gotquestions.org/dunamis -meaning.html (accessed March 11, 2015).
3. Ricky L. Johnson, "Midian, Midianites," *Holman Bible Dictionary*, StudyLight.org, http://www.studylight.org/ dictionaries/hbd/view.cgi?n=4300 (accessed March 11, 2015).
4. BehindtheName.com, "Ishmael," http://www.behindthe-name.com/name/ishmael (accessed March 11, 2015).
5. BehindtheName.com, "Reuben," http://www.behindthe-name.com/name/reuben (accessed March 11, 2015).

CHAPTER 9
BE BRAVE

1. Spine-health.com, "Scheuermann's Disease of the Thoracic and Lumbar Spine," http://www.spine-health.com /conditions/spinal-deformities/scheuermanns-disease -thoracic-and-lumbar-spine (accessed March 11, 2015).
2. Amanda Cook, "You Make Me Brave," Bethel Music Publishing, 2013.

ABOUT THE AUTHOR
KAREN SCHATZLINE
REMNANT MINISTRIES INTERNATIONAL

Karen Schatzline is an international Evangelist and Author who travels extensively around the world ministering the Gospel. She is the Co-Founder of Remnant Ministries International. Karen leads with a heart of transformation for the hurting, and she is best known for her messages of hope, freedom and intimacy with the Father. Her ministry gatherings are always invaded with the tangible presence of God! She is known for using humor, straight talk and relative topics to convey her messages of hope. Karen believes that it is time for the bride of Christ to rise-up and walk out the authority God has given each of us to overcome the lies of the enemy. Karen has appeared many times on Christian Television Networks such as CTN, TBN and Daystar.

Karen makes her home in Birmingham, AL along with her husband, Evangelist/ Author Pat Schatzline and daughter Abigail. Their son Nate, daughter-in-love Adrienne and grandson Jackson live in CA where they are Youth Pastors.

LISTEN TO MORE OF KAREN'S MESSAGSE ONLINE VIA OUR PODCAST & ITUNES

WWW.REMNANT.INTERNATIONAL

WWW.DEHYDRATEDBOOK.COM
WWW.REMNANT.INTERNATIONAL
INFO@REMNANT.INTERNATIONAL
205-874-9401

FOLLOW KAREN ON TWITTER & INSTAGRAM: @KARENSCHATZLINE

AND DEHYDRATED ON TWITTER AT: @DEHYDRATEDBOOK

EMPOWERED
TO RADICALLY CHANGE
YOUR WORLD